BUDDHISM
in the Tibetan Tradition:
A GUIDE

BUDDHISM
in the Tibetan Tradition: A GUIDE

GESHE KELSANG GYATSO

Translated by
Tenzin P. Phunrabpa

Edited by
R. F. and M. R. Lister

With a Foreword by
H. H. The Dalai Lama

Routledge & Kegan Paul
London and New York

First published in 1984
Reprinted in 1986
by Routledge & Kegan Paul plc

11 New Fetter Lane, London EC4P 4EE

Published in the USA by
Routledge & Kegan Paul Inc.
in association with Methuen Inc.
29 West 35th Street, New York, NY10001.

Set in Plantin, 10 on 12pt,
by Print Origination & Publicity Services, Aldershot,
and printed in Great Britain
by Billing & Sons Ltd, Worcester

Library of Congress Cataloging in Publication Data

Kelsang Gyatso.

Buddhism in Tibetan Tradition: a guide
1. Buddhism—China—Tibet. 2. Buddhism—Doctrines.
I. Lister, R. F. II. Lister, M. R. III. Title.
BQ7604.K45 1984 294.3'923 83-24622

British Library CIP available

ISBN 0-7102-0242-3 (U.S. : pbk)

CONTENTS

ILLUSTRATIONS

by Andy Weber

FOREWORD

Very often people who are interested in studying Tibetan Buddhism are dissuaded from doing so because they cannot always find books that are written in a way that they can easily follow. This is particularly true for people who have to spend most of their lives making a living, the stress and strain of which leaves them little time for anything else. At the same time, our present life style does not help to solve our problems, and in fact, the only sensible way to live a less tense life seems to be by developing our mental and spiritual capacities.

I am, therefore, happy that Geshe Kelsang Gyatso has attempted to present the basic teachings of Lord Buddha in a manner that people can relate to and put them into practice in their daily lives. I would like to thank the translator and editors for their efforts.

H. H. The Dalai Lama

EDITORS' INTRODUCTION

This book has been compiled from a series of lectures given by the Venerable Geshe Kelsang Gyatso at the Madhyamaka Centre in York, England. The lectures were translated into English by Tenzin P. Phunrabpa.

The editors sincerely thank Geshe Kelsang Gyatso for the boundless compassion and wisdom with which he transmitted these teachings. The editors also wish to express their appreciation to the translator, to the students of the Madhyamaka Centre who diligently transcribed the lectures, and to Jonathan Landaw, Mariana Libano and Martin Wills for their many helpful comments and suggestions about the text. Finally, the editors would like to thank the many other people who assisted in the preparation of this book in numerous ways.

It is hoped that *Buddhism in the Tibetan Tradition: A Guide* will provide a clear and basic introduction to Tibetan Buddhism for those new to the subject as well as offering some new insights for the more advanced student. Unfamiliar words and terminology are explained in the Glossary.

Chapter 1

WHAT IS DHARMA?

All of us have attained a human body which is something even more valuable than Aladdin's wish-granting lamp — if we don't misuse it. If we do misuse our body, then there is no great value in having a human form. Misusing our human body is similar to someone who has a large fortune but instead of using this wealth to benefit others, misuses it by harming them.

It is extremely important to use the potential of our human body correctly. The reason why this is so important is because the human form is very rare and meaningful. It doesn't matter that there are many human beings; each person has only one body. As everyone knows, a single person cannot keep two bodies. Although one person can keep more than one house or car, he or she can keep only one body. Furthermore, if our car or other possessions should be damaged we can replace them; however, if our body deteriorates it is impossible to buy or borrow another. Therefore this human body is our rarest possession.

Not only is our body extremely rare, it also has great meaning. This signifies that we can achieve ultimate happiness by using our human body properly. What is the method for achieving such ultimate happiness? — Only Dharma.

In general, Dharma refers to the teachings of the Buddha, but the actual Dharma is the inner realizations which directly protect living beings from their sufferings. If we do not contemplate the nature of Dharma, then we will not understand the usefulness, capabilities, and functions of Dharma; and we will not be able to judge whether or not we need Dharma.

The word 'Dharma' is a Sanskrit term which means literally 'that which holds'. It is Dharma which holds living beings back from sufferings, fears and dangers. However, in order to become free from our own problems and sufferings, we need to exert great effort to achieve

Dharma realizations. In a similar way, a medicine may be very effective, but a sick person who fails to take it will not be cured.

Dharma is like a medicine, the Buddha is like a doctor, and the community of Dharma practitioners are like nurses. Just as a sick person needs a skilful doctor, the correct medicine and helpful nurses, we need to rely on the doctor-like Buddha, medicine-like Dharma and nurse-like spiritual community if we wish to be free from our sufferings.

How does Dharma protect us directly? If we gain any spiritual experiences, these experiences will definitely solve some of our inner problems. For example, if we gain the realization and experience of patience, this will solve all our problems which arise from anger. In the same way, if we achieve the realization of compassion, this will solve all of our problems arising from jealousy. And ultimately, if we gain the intuitive realization of emptiness — the ultimate nature of all phenomena — this will solve all of our problems and eliminate our sufferings. In summary, Dharma realizations eradicate our inner problems and lead us to temporal and ultimate peace.

In addition to these qualities, Dharma has the quality of being our actual refuge. Some people may think that their wealth and possessions or their relatives and friends can solve their problems and help give them mental peace. Thus, they regard these things as a refuge from suffering. Of course, sometimes possessions, relatives or friends can solve our problems and give us some happiness. But there are many problems they cannot solve; sometimes they even create more problems and suffering for us. We cannot rely on possessions, relatives or friends to help us in every situation. Therefore these are not our actual refuge. Besides Dharma, we cannot find any actual refuge.

Traditionally, at the beginning of a discourse lamas give a preliminary introduction before beginning the teaching. The purpose of this is to establish a correct motivation on the part of both the teacher and the disciples. In keeping with this tradition, a verse given by one Buddhist master as advice to his friend, a king, will be explained here.

'Your present body is as if you borrowed it from someone.'

This means that the source of our body belongs to others. Our body developed from the union of our father's sperm and mother's egg. Consciousness entered into that union and then gradually our body developed.

At death we have no power to carry our body with us into a future life. We cannot prevent the decay and dissolution of our body after death.

Thus, it is said that the consciousness is like a visitor or guest in a guest house — the body. It is important to remember and contemplate upon this because of our strong clinging to our body. This verse is just as relevant to us today as it was to the king to whom it was first delivered.

The consciousness leaves the body at death like a tourist leaving his guest house and going on to other places. In the same way that ordinary people can move to a new house, some highly realized beings can move into another body at will. We should contemplate the inevitability of leaving our body at death, knowing that we are like a traveller in this life and not permanently connected to our present body.

Thinking that we will be here forever leads to many problems. The ego tries to protect itself by surrounding itself with all the worldly accessories of this life, such as possessions and mundane achievements. We forget that at the time of death it is necessary to leave all these things behind.

We cannot hope to benefit much from Dharma if we just sit and listen or read it passively, as if we were watching television. We can obtain some advantages from an intellectual study of Dharma, but to obtain the full benefits we must live Dharma with all aspects of our being and know it truly through experience.

'Even though your body is like a guest house,
If you practise Dharma you will receive many fruits.'

This means that we should use our body, which we have only for a short while, to practise Dharma. We ought not to waste this precious vessel or human body which can enable us to reach Enlightenment. Misused, our body can commit all kinds of negative actions instead of helping us along the spiritual path. But through practising Dharma, we can achieve the full potential of our human form.

Through Dharma practice there are three kinds of meaning to be achieved. The highest meaning is to reach full Enlightenment, Buddhahood, in this life. The middle kind of meaning is to achieve self-liberation from samsaric fears and sufferings. The lowest meaning is to try to obtain a peaceful mind, to solve one's inner problems, and not to be reborn in the lower realms. Thus, the teacher advised his friend the king to practise Dharma, aiming at one of these three scopes or levels of meaning.

We human beings have the opportunity to practise Dharma because of our precious human body. Knowing this and seeing the extensive benefits which can be obtained, we should try to understand and practise Dharma. The following chapters give some explanations about how to do this.

Chapter 2

THE GOOD HEART

When the great Buddhist teacher Atisha was living in Tibet, many people used to come to see him. Whenever Atisha met anyone he would inquire,

'Do you have a good heart?'

Usually when we meet someone we ask,

'How are you?',

but Atisha asked a more profound question. He recognized that anyone who has a kind heart is a good person. When Atisha advised anyone he would say,

'Try to cultivate a good heart.'

Whether we commit positive or negative actions depends upon the nature of our heart or mind. A bad or negative mind will lead us to commit negative actions and, equally, a good or wholesome mind will lead us to perform positive actions. The result of negative actions will be many problems; the result of good actions will be happiness. Through the force of having a good heart we will obtain temporary happiness. The ultimate happiness of Enlightenment is also achieved through the force of the good heart.

Even happiness in our family relationships depends upon our having a good heart. A family's love and compassion is based on the good hearts of its members. For example, for a couple, having a good relationship depends upon their having good hearts. If the hearts of both the husband and wife are negative, suffering will result. Thus, in order to attain happiness – from insignificant temporary happiness to the ultimate happiness of Buddhahood – we must try to develop a good heart.

We should carefully investigate how to generate a good heart. First of all, we must be able to distinguish between good and bad states of mind. Then we should try to eliminate our negative states of mind and increase our positive ones. Any kind of mind which disturbs our inner peace is called a negative or bad mind. Negative thoughts such as resentment, jealousy, anger, greed, wishing to harm others, holding wrong views and bad attitudes, wrong discernment and faithlessness disturb our mind and cause us problems. These thoughts destroy our happiness and cause us misery.

It is easy to see how a negative mind causes one to experience suffering. For instance, a person may have a very positive mind but then develops anger. After having a calm mind, if anger suddenly arises, that person no longer has a happy or peaceful mind. No matter how much delicious food is served to such an angry person, he cannot enjoy it. The angry mind in effect steals one's happiness and peace. Everyone who develops anger or hatred experiences unhappiness. The result of anger is the creation of problems. Bad actions such as quarrelling, fighting and killing are caused by anger. Because of these negative actions much suffering is experienced.

A jealous or envious mind also creates problems. The more we have a jealous mind, the more we are unhappy and cannot find any peace. Likewise, the more attachment we have, the more problems we experience. At the moment most of our problems arise because of attachment. A thief, for example, may be sent to prison for the whole of his life because of his attachment. He first became attached to someone else's possessions and then, motivated by attachment, stole and perhaps killed in order to obtain them. The result of his attachment is imprisonment and unbearable suffering. Also, in terms of family and personal relationships, intense attachment can lead to problems such as overpossessiveness.

The Buddhist master Vasubandhu used many examples to show how attachment creates suffering. His first example was that flies have a very strong attachment to pleasing odours. Yet when they try to land on food, humans kill them. Moths are attached to beautiful forms such as light. When they see light, they regard it as a very pleasant place. Moths develop strong attachment and desire to be inside an attractive light such as a candle-flame. They try to enter into the light and finally die.

Another example of the disadvantages of strong desire is the attachment which fish have to food. Fishermen put a small piece of food on top of a hook. When fish see or smell that food, they bite the hook. As a result they die. Some wild animals are attached to beautiful sounds.

Hunters used to play the mouth organ or flute to make animals approach them. Then the hunters would kill the animals.

According to Vasubandhu, some living beings die from attachment to visual form or sound, taste, smell or touch. But human beings have strong attachment to all of these five sense objects. As these examples demonstrate, the negative mind of attachment is the source of many problems. Although we all have negative minds such as attachment, as human beings we have the precious opportunity to practise methods to stop negative minds from arising and to prevent the resultant suffering.

What, then, constitute good or positive minds? Good minds include beneficial intentions towards others, compassion, loving-kindness, generosity, moral discipline, tolerance, patience, and the joyful desire to practise Dharma. A mind which wishes to gain concentration, a mind which wishes to realize emptiness or to gain the renunciation of samsara, and a mind which wishes to attain Enlightenment for the sake of all sentient beings are all positive minds. These thoughts are classified as good thoughts because they give happiness to oneself and also produce happiness for others. These positive minds have great power to solve or reduce our problems.

The more we cultivate a good heart, the fewer will be our negative thoughts. Our difficulties will also become fewer. The more we develop a good heart, the greater will be our happiness. Sometimes it is inspiring to consider the lives of realized yogis of the past. These yogis developed happiness through the force of the good heart. By training their minds the yogis achieved high mental development. When the yogis encountered adverse circumstances, they transformed these into the spiritual path. Unlike worldly people who experience suffering when they meet difficulties, the ancient yogis spent their lives from joy to joy. As the great Buddhist yogi Shantideva said:

> 'I never become discouraged because I am travelling the path to Enlightenment which leads from joy to joy.'

If we try to develop a good heart we will naturally find some inner peace. Without cultivating a good heart we will never find pure peace. If we do not have internal peace, even world peace cannot bring peace to our own mind. It is our duty to find our own internal mental peace.

Pure happiness and the development of mental peace cannot be achieved solely by concentrating on material things. In order to obtain or achieve material rewards we must exert great effort. While we are exerting this effort we experience more suffering than happiness. And, after achieving material goals, we find that they cannot satisfy our inner needs. Therefore we need spiritual or Dharma practices.

Especially during a degenerate age when there is much fighting and many dangers, we need to devote a large amount of energy to Dharma practice. But even during this degenerate time we are fortunate in having the opportunity to make our mind happy by training in Dharma.

TRANSFORMING NEGATIVE MINDS

At first it is very difficult to transform a negative mind into a positive one. For instance, if someone has an angry mind it is impossible to transform this angry mind into love suddenly. Any negative mind which develops cannot immediately be transformed into a wholesome mind. Just as black woollen cloth is very difficult to dye yellow without first removing the black colour, we must first destroy or overcome a negative mind before a positive mind can arise. Thus, if negative thoughts arise, we should first of all try to overcome them. Then we should try to transform our thoughts into positive or beneficial ones.

There are two methods for transforming negative thoughts into positive thoughts. The first method is to overcome negative conceptual thoughts. The second method is actually to try to develop a good heart. Initially, we should put great effort into abandoning negative thoughts. If we practise Dharma it is not very hard to destroy negative conceptual thoughts including anger or hatred. These thoughts can fairly easily be destroyed temporarily, but it is very hard to uproot and eliminate negative conceptual thoughts completely. Until we gain an intuitive realization of emptiness, it is not possible to destroy the root of negative thoughts. But there are many ways to overcome negative conceptual thoughts temporarily.

Although no one wishes to experience an unhappy mind, unhappy and upset states of mind frequently arise. Sometimes an unhappy mind arises from attachment, anger, jealousy, miserliness or greed. Miserliness, for instance, leads to problems which cause unhappiness. If someone spends a great deal of money on expensive food and then later feels regret that his money is gone, this creates an unhappy state of mind. If it were not for the miserliness, unhappiness would not have arisen.

Sometimes, by thinking of future rebirths, an individual can become upset. Through worrying that his or her future life will be difficult or impoverished, unhappiness develops. Owing to attachment to this present life, thinking that it is very important and precious, mental distress occurs. As long as a person thinks only of himself, of his own welfare and his present selfish concerns, his inner unhappiness will never end.

It is necessary to achieve the intuitive realization of emptiness in order to destroy completely all of one's negative conceptual thoughts, but there are many methods to solve or reduce problems temporarily. First, we should know that an unhappy mind does not arise automatically; it depends upon causes. Each negative thought has a different set of causes. Negative conceptual thoughts have two types of causes which arise simultaneously. One type of cause of a negative thought is the object of that thought. The second type of cause is our internal impure mounting energy winds (prana). The energy winds flow through our body in channels and the functioning of our mind depends upon these winds. Energy winds are responsible for our memory and our conceptual thoughts.

In most of the Tantric texts it is stated that we develop negative thoughts because of impure energy winds. Although we now develop many negative thoughts, these thoughts are not permanent. The negative conceptualizations like anger are only temporary, caused by impure energy winds and meeting an external object of anger. Such delusions are not dissolved into our root mind, the very subtle mind which continues from life to life.

If we do not have any impure energy winds, just meeting an external object cannot cause anger to develop. Buddhas, for example, never develop anger. They do encounter external objects, but they do not have internal impure energy winds. When Shakyamuni Buddha was alive, Devadata, a very evil-minded person, constantly tried to harm him. But Buddha, free from impure energy winds, never developed any anger toward Devadatta.

On the other hand, if we do not meet an object of anger — even though we do possess internal impure energy winds — anger will not arise. From this we can see that there are two methods to use to overcome an angry mind. One method is to try to stop the impure energy winds from arising; the other is to try to forget the object of anger.

The same two methods are useful for overcoming other negative thoughts. To prevent attachment we should try to stop the arising of impure energy winds and then try to forget the object of our attachment. If we wish to conquer self-grasping, we should meditate on stopping the development of impure energy winds and then meditate in order to forget the object of our self-grasping. Thus we have two meditations to do: first, to stop impure energy winds from arising; and second, to forget the object of our negative thoughts.

These two meditations solve our problems temporarily, but not finally or ultimately. After we complete these two meditations it is still possible for our negative thoughts to arise again. If this happens we should repeat the same two meditations.

Secret Mantra or Tantra contains methods through which we can stop impure energy winds from arising. Most of our impure energy winds flow through our left or right channel. Our body has many channels, but there are three principal ones: the central, right and left channels. The most important is the central channel. At the moment energy winds cannot flow through our central channel. They flow through our right and left channels instead. But the energy winds that flow in our right and left channels are impure or defiled energy winds which cause delusions or negative conceptions to develop. Owing to this, we should practise the meditation explained below in order to prevent the energy winds from flowing in our right and left channels and causing deluded minds to arise.

Meditation on purifying defiled energy winds

Through the nine-breath or nine-round purification practice we should try to expel our defiled energy winds. The defiled energy winds which help to develop strong delusions flow principally in the right channel. Therefore we should try to obstruct the right channel. We should begin by placing the tip or our left thumb against the base of our left ring finger, and then make a fist by closing the four fingers over the thumb. With this left fist we should press on the right side of our rib cage so that our fist rests at the level of the right elbow, in line with the armpit.

Next we should make a similar fist with our right hand, but with the index finger extended. With the back or nail side of the extended right index finger we press the left nostril closed. We then inhale smoothly through our right nostril, visualizing that all the inspiring strength of the Buddhas and Bodhisattvas enters into us through the right nostril in the form of radiant white light. We should then feel that the Buddhas' and Bodhisattvas' blessings have blessed our mind. Our inhalation should be a full, deep breath and we should hold this breath for as long as possible.

To exhale, we move our right index finger over to our right nostril, pressing it closed with the front of the right index finger. Then we should exhale all the air gently in three equal successive breaths through the left nostril. As we exhale, we should visualize that all impure energy winds, particularly those from the left side of our body, are expelled in the form of black light.

With our right index finger still holding our right nostril closed, we now inhale through our left nostril slowly, smoothly and deeply, visualizing that all the inspiring strength of the Buddhas and Bodhisattvas streams into us in the form of radiant white light. Again we think that the Buddhas' and Bodhisattvas' blessings have blessed our mind. We should remain with this experience, holding our breath until we become uncomfortable.

In order to exhale, we transfer our right index finger again to the left nostril. We exhale fully all impure energy winds in the form of black light in three equal breaths from our right nostril. This purifies our impure energy winds, especially those from the right side of our body.

The last three rounds are done through both nostrils simultaneously. Our hands can now be placed in the meditation position – palms upward, right hand resting on the left, and thumbs touching. The hands are placed in this position close to our body, just below the navel.

We inhale smoothly through both nostrils with the same visualization of white light as before, then exhale in three equal breaths which we visualize in the form of black light. After we inhale, we should think that the Buddhas' and Bodhisattvas' blessings entered our mind, making it very calm. As we exhale we should think that from our left and right channels and from all subsidiary channels the impure energy winds depart. When the final ninth exhalation has been completed, we should think that all the energy winds in our body have been purified. Our body feels very flexible and comfortable.

After finishing the nine rounds of purifying defiled energy winds (which can be done several times in succession), we may begin whatever is to be our main meditation for that session. For example, if we are interested in doing breath meditation, we should turn our concentration to the subtle sensation inside our nostrils. As we inhale and exhale normally, there is a subtle sensation inside our nose. We should meditate on that sensation single-pointedly as a general sensation inside our nose, without locating it in any one place.

The nine-round meditation is very helpful in preventing negative thoughts by purifying impure energy winds. If we do this practice every day it will be beneficial. At the moment we are unused to this practice and at first we may not get quick results from it. But by becoming accustomed to this meditation, it becomes very useful in overcoming our negative thoughts. This meditation also helps to overcome anxiety and other types of unhappy minds.

This entire practice can be very beneficial, but its result depends on the way in which it is practised. For instance, if someone is given a car but does not know how to drive it, that car will be useless even if it is in good working order. The same is true for this meditation: although the meditation can be very helpful, if we do not perform it properly and conscientiously it cannot help us. But if we do this nine-round meditation every day it helps to calm our mind. Then we have a great opportunity to develop positive minds, such as love, compassion and bodhicitta. Otherwise, it is very difficult to develop positive minds while we still have negative conceptions.

Forgetting the object of negative thoughts

The second meditation for overcoming negative minds is meditation to forget the object of our negative thoughts. In general, any wholesome meditation that we perform helps us to forget the object of negative thoughts. If, for instance, someone has strong attachment to wealth, visualizing and meditating on Buddha's form will help him or her to forget the object of attachment. Through developing strong concentration on Buddha's form, the object of attachment will naturally be forgotten. Similarly, if we have strong anger, visualizing Buddha helps us to forget the object. If this meditation becomes very successful our anger will be pacified.

At present our mind cannot focus on two different objects simultaneously. We cannot concentrate both on the object of our anger and on the object of our wholesome meditation. If we concentrate strongly on one, then naturally we forget the other. Therefore if we have a very good meditation, any object of our negative thoughts will be forgotten. The breathing meditation outlined earlier will also help us to forget the object of our delusion. If we forget the object, then our negative minds, such as anger, will be reduced. Our mind will become peaceful. Thus, we can use any positive meditation on Buddha, on love, on emptiness and so forth to forget the object of our negative thoughts.

Through the force of these two types of meditation — purifying our internal energy winds and forgetting the object of delusion — we can destroy all our negative thoughts. After eliminating our negative thoughts, we should try to cultivate a positive mind. It is as if we have taken out the black colour from the woollen cloth and now it is easy to dye it yellow. Now that we have destroyed our negative conceptions it is easy to achieve realizations such as compassion and bodhicitta.

THE THREE PRINCIPAL ASPECTS OF THE PATH

In the Buddhist teachings there are three main spiritual paths: renunciation, bodhicitta or the altruistic mind aspiring to attain Enlightenment for the benefit of others, and the correct view of emptiness. Without depending on these three principal aspects of the path to Enlightenment, it is impossible to reach Buddhahood. Within the three principal aspects, we should first try to achieve renunciation. Renunciation here does not mean giving up our family, friends and so forth; it means wishing to escape from cyclic existence — the uncontrolled cycle of birth, death and rebirth.

If we consider the fear, suffering and danger which we have experienced up to now and also consider the fear, suffering and danger which we will definitely experience in the future, we will see that there is no place in samsara or cyclic existence where these problems do not exist. For example, no one wishes to experience old age, but it arrives naturally. Illness, death and other miseries also arise naturally so that we have no choice but to face them. If we develop the continuous and spontaneous wish to escape from cyclic existence, this is called renunciation.

Human beings have a great opportunity to achieve the mind of renunciation. Renunciation is a wholesome mind particular to human beings. No animal, for example, is capable of wishing to escape from cyclic existence.

Up to now we have seen and experienced samsaric fears and sufferings, but we have not developed the wish to escape from them. This is because we have not met the instructors who can guide us to nirvana or liberation. If there were no chance to escape from samsara it would be pointless to cultivate renunciation and the desire for liberation. But it is possible to escape from samsara and there are many methods for accomplishing this.

Many people feel that cyclic existence is like a paradise and they plan to remain in samsara for a long time. Many people develop strong attachment to cyclic existence; their main object of concentration is samsara. Pure Dharma practitioners, however, see samsara as a prison and develop a strong desire to escape from it. They cultivate the precious thought of renunciation.

Renunciation may be hard to develop right now. First of all we have to see the faults of cyclic existence. The reason that Buddhist teachings explain the prevalence of suffering is to enable us to realize renunciation. Otherwise, it would not be necessary to meditate upon suffering.

If we have great wisdom, it may seem as though we don't need to read books in order to understand suffering and neither do we need to receive instructions on misery or dissatisfaction. We experience suffering ourself; we also see that others are experiencing suffering. We know that the future will bring many experiences of suffering for ourself and others. Thus, the great Tibetan yogi Milarepa said:

> 'I don't need these black letters to read. I perceive all appearances as Dharma teachings. All appearances teach me the faults of cyclic existence. All appearances teach me death awareness and the profound view of emptiness.'

If we are very skilful like Milarepa, whatever we experience teaches us Dharma.

It may be difficult for us to understand this. We have to think, meditate, and improve our mind. If we do this we have great prospects for reaching spiritual realizations. Then we will derive great meaning from our human existence, from our precious human rebirth. Should we not practise Dharma, we will one day be faced with our own death and find that our life has been meaningless. We will have wasted the potentiality of the human form. The only thing we can carry with us to our next life is the virtuous or non-virtuous karma we have accumulated. We cannot bring our relatives, friends or possessions. Therefore, it is important to practise Dharma continuously. By depending on Dharma we can attain the spiritual realizations which will help us in future lives.

Our Dharma practice needs sustained effort day by day and year by year. For some people spiritual realizations may develop quickly, like striking a match. Others may find realizations difficult to achieve. But if we practise, Dharma teachings will become more clear and more relevant to our life. At first we may be confused by Dharma teachings because they are very profound. Dharma may be different from our habitual ways of thinking; it may seem strange the first time we hear it. However, by contemplating, meditating and reflecting on Dharma, we can feel that our mind and Dharma have mixed together, that our mind has been absorbed into the Dharma.

If a person feels that there is a great distance between his or her mind and Dharma, it is hard to reach realizations. When we feel that our mind and Dharma are mixing or meeting there is great hope for attaining spiritual realizations. Some people may hear Dharma teachings for many years, but do not achieve realizations because their minds and Dharma have not really mixed.

At present there is a wide gap between our mind and Dharma. What we have to do is to bring our mind and Dharma closer and closer together. After some time we will feel our mind dissolve into the Dharma. Then we can think more deeply about Dharma and attain realizations.

Chapter 3

IMPERMANENCE

There are two kinds of impermanence. The first is gross impermanence and the second kind is subtle impermanence. Although gross impermanence is generally very easy to recognize, we are rarely aware of the gross changes which are continually taking place around us. One example of gross impermanence is the way that we change throughout our life. When we were born into the world we were small and helpless. We were unable to eat coarse food and totally depended upon our parents. A few months after birth we began to change dramatically in appearance and to acquire new skills. After one or more years we were able to walk, to talk coherently, and to eat coarse food. Infancy turns into youth, youth into middle age, middle age into old age, and old age eventually leads to the most vivid example of impermanence — death.

In general, everyone can understand this type of impermanence and therefore no further logical reasoning is needed to establish its existence. It is for this reason that this first kind of impermanence is gross impermanence

Gross impermanence pervades not only all sentient beings, but also all inanimate things.* For instance, when a house has just been built we refer to it as being new. After several months the house becomes a little older, and after several years it becomes older still, until eventually it crumbles away. A flower is at first fresh and beautiful. But after only a few days the flower will lose its freshness, its petals will begin to fall, and finally it will wither and decay. Even the world system in which we live was once new. From its beginning until now it has become many millions of years old, but eventually it too will be destroyed completely.

*See glossary for this special usage of the word 'thing'.

All such changes are examples of gross impermanence. Our world system and all the beings and things within it are of the nature of impermanence. We cannot find one human being who never becomes old and will never die and we cannot find any thing which will remain permanently in existence without eventually perishing.

Although we can all understand gross impermanence very easily, we rarely contemplate its meaning or the effects it has on us. If we seriously contemplated the effects of gross impermanence, this would inevitably bring about changes in our way of thinking. We would develop a different feeling for gross impermanence and the way that it functions in our life.

We usually regard the things which surround us, as well as ourself, to be permanent. However, this is a mistaken view. By meditating on impermanence, we can attain internal realizations and develop a special feeling about impermanence. We should try to cultivate this special feeling.

Meditating on impermanence causes our mind and Dharma to mix together. Without meditating on impermanence and developing an understanding of it, our mind and Dharma will never become very close. We may understand impermanence intellectually, but without meditating on it, even though we may have received many other teachings, our mind and Dharma will not readily mix. If we consider carefully, we will find that impermanence is the best method to transform our mind into pure Dharma.

For many people it is difficult to develop an interest in and the wish to practise Dharma. One of the main reasons for this is that we feel and think we will remain on this earth forever. Holding this view of our own permanence, we are usually only interested in acquiring that which will add to our well-being and security in this life. The stronger the feeling of permanence is, the less interest there will be in integrating our life with the Dharma. It is for this reason that it is said that whenever we practise Dharma, the first step is to be mindful of impermanence.

Contemplating impermanence, thus, is essential to Dharma practice. Because the most powerful example of impermanence is death, it is useful to examine it. At first it may be difficult to face the thought that we must eventually die; but if we are not mindful of death it becomes very easy to fall under the influence of the thought which deceives our mind into feeling that we are permanent.

Although there are many instances of gross impermanence which can be observed, meditation on death is an especially effective cause to practise Dharma purely. The Buddha's first step to Enlightenment was meditating on impermanence. It was through the force of understanding impermanence that the Buddha developed a strong motivation to practise pure Dharma, and it was through his Dharma practice that he finally attained Enlightenment. When the Buddha first gave teachings, turning the wheel of Dharma, he explained impermanence. The Buddha said that impermanence is the best meditation for beginners.

Most of our problems arise from thinking that everything — including ourself — is permanent. If we have the realization that everything including ourself is of the nature of impermanence, then we will experience fewer problems. Thus, meditating on impermanence helps to solve our temporary problems. It also helps our spiritual practice to become very pure. Meditation on death and impermanence is the best method to dispel laziness. It aids us in reaching Enlightenment quickly.

Some people may think that impermanence is a very elementary meditation suitable only for beginners. But this is not the case: even very highly realized beings should meditate on impermanence. Tantric practitioners used to keep human bones, such as thigh bones, and objects made from human bones, such as skull-cups, in order to remind themselves of impermanence. If a Tantric practitioner does not remember impermanence, then that Tantric practice becomes just for the sake of this life. Practising Tantra just for the sake of this life is not a pure practice. Thus, meditating on impermanence is important for all levels of Dharma practice.

If we know how to meditate on impermanence this has special benefits. It is easier to develop an internal feeling for impermanence than for other objects of meditation. This is because there are many direct examples of impermanence which we can meditate upon. Therefore, meditating on impermanence is more powerful than other meditation techniques.

MEDITATION ON DEATH AND IMPERMANENCE

The meditation on death has three roots, nine reasons and three determinations. If we know these roots, reasons and determinations, our meditation on death and impermanence will be very powerful. The three roots of the meditation are:

1 Death is definite
2 The time of death is indefinite
3 At the time of death only Dharma can help us.

The nine reasons which were explained by Je Tsong Khapa are the method to receive the experience of the meditation on death and impermanence. Although everyone knows that death is definite, only a few people have received the experience of death and impermanence meditation. By meditating on the three roots and nine reasons we can receive this experience.

1 Death is definite

The first of the three reasons why death is definite is because the process of death cannot be avoided by any method. Until we reach nirvana or Enlightenment we cannot overcome death no matter how hard we try. We cannot bribe death, fight or escape from it. Even a doctor as skilled as the Buddha cannot prevent our death. Because we were born into cyclic existence it is definite that we have to die. We should conclude from this that it is definite that I, myself, have to die.

If we develop a new positive feeling through this meditation, we should then try to concentrate on this feeling. Meditation means focusing the mind on a wholesome object without forgetting it. If we develop a strong wish to receive some meaning out of our life by practising Dharma, our meditation on impermanence is going well. Likewise, if we find that our clinging to permanence is being reduced and that we are experiencing fewer internal problems, this also means that our meditation is successful.

The second reason why death is definite is because the length of our life span decreases with every passing moment and cannot be extended. With each minute the time that remains to us in this life becomes shorter and shorter. No matter what we are doing — working, resting or sleeping — our life is ebbing away. Even while we are reading this chapter our life is passing by. Life is like a candle which quickly burns down. When we glance at the candle it does not seem to be becoming shorter; but actually it is continually burning away. Buddha compared our life to a flash of lightning: the lightning strikes and is swiftly gone. In the same way, life passes very quickly and is soon over.

Thinking in this way, we should come to the conclusion:

'It is certain that I will die because my life is becoming shorter

> with each passing moment. There is no time during which my life is not ebbing away. It is as if I were rolling a stone down a high mountain. The stone never stops in its journey, but keeps on travelling every instant until it reaches the bottom.'

The great Buddhist master Shantideva said that with every moment one's life is passing away and there is no way to increase one's life span. Whereas when other things are used up they can be replaced, there is no way to replace life once it has passed by. Even if we are fortunate enough to live for eighty years, with every instant that eighty years is being used up and cannot be extended. This life is constantly heading toward its end.

In the Sutra texts it is said that ever since birth we are moving toward death. We are continually coming closer and closer to the time when we will meet death. Contemplating these reasons, we should realize:

'It is certain that I will die.'

We should then decide that in view of the constant shortening of our life and the certainty of death, we will try to receive some meaning from life before the time of death arrives.

The third reason is that death is definite even though we have no time to practise Dharma. We may devote little time to practising Dharma and cultivating our inner spiritual development, but still we must face death. We should investigate how much time we devote to practising Dharma purely. Worldly activities take up most of our time. From morning until evening we are busy with our work, preparing meals, seeking amusements and so forth. Do we practise Dharma even when we have spare time? Usually very little. Then our life ends and we face death even though we have not practised Dharma very much. Although we have not received much meaning from this life, death will come. In order to receive the experience from this third reason we have to examine it in terms of our own experience. We have to think of what we do from morning until evening and see that there is not much time when we practise Dharma. We should think how we will feel if we have spent our life like this and then death approaches.

In this way we can try to use this method to receive the experience of the meditation. All of these reasons are the means to gain the experience of this impermanence meditation. Through these three reasons we should try to receive the experience that death is definite.

For each of the three roots there is a corresponding determination that we should make. After the meditation that death is definite we should decide: 'I will practise Dharma.' This determination is the fruit of the meditation, and if we really decide this it shows that we have received the experience of the meditation.

2 The time of death is indefinite

The first of the three reasons for this root is that the life span of beings on this earth is unfixed. That is, there is no way of knowing how long we will live. There is no difference between young and old: the young may die before the old. Some beings die in the womb, some after birth, and some live to old age. There is no definite order of old and young in terms of death.

Equally, there is no difference between the healthy and the unhealthy in terms of death. Some unhealthy people live for a long time whereas some healthy people die in accidents or unexpectedly before those who are ill die. People who are confined to hospitals may outlive those who continue their normal lives. Therefore we should think that the time of death is uncertain because it does not depend upon our state of health. Likewise, there is no certainty that the old will die before the young.

The second reason why the time of death is indefinite is because there are many conditions which lead to death and very few conditions which support life. Life depends on having certain conditions such as water, food, air to breathe, and a particular level of temperature in which to live. If we lack these conditions or meet unfavourable conditions like extreme cold, death will follow. Thus, the time of death is uncertain because there are many conditions unfavourable to life and we cannot be sure that we will never encounter these conditions.

The third reason why death is indefinite is because our body is very delicate. It is not necessary to be attacked with powerful weapons to be killed. Because our body is very delicate there are many ways to meet death. Snakebites, tiny amounts of poison, or swallowing contaminated food or water can easily cause death. Therefore we should think:

> 'Because my body is so fragile, the cause of my death could occur at any time. The time of my death is totally indefinite.'

In summary, we don't know which will come first — tomorrow or our next life. It is possible that our next life will come even before our next meal. We should think deeply about the causes which lead to death. We can see that many people who go out happily in the morning will never return home.

We cannot predict what will happen in the future. Although we can remember what happened in the past, we are unaware of what tomorrow and the day after hold for us. Our future is completely uncertain and we can never rule out the possibility of dying.

Among the three roots, thinking that the time of death is indefinite is the most powerful. If we continue to think

> 'I will not die today,'

this thought deceives us. Certainly one day we will die.

For instance, if we know that an enemy is coming to kill us during this month but we are not sure on which date he is coming, we will be very cautious. However, if every day we think that today is not the day when he is coming, then we will be taken by surprise when he arrives and we will be defeated. But if every day we think that today will be the day when our enemy is coming, we will be prepared for him. Likewise, if we know that death can arrive at any time during our life, we will be prepared when it does arrive.

Through contemplating these three reasons why the time of our death is uncertain, we should make a strong determination to receive some meaning or spiritual experience while we have the opportunity. We will have to die empty-handed if we have not gained any Dharma experience from life. We should conclude:

> 'Since it is true that I may die at any time, I will practise Dharma right now.'

3 At the time of death only Dharma can help

The first reason why only Dharma can aid us at the time of death is that our possessions are useless at that time. Nothing we own or possess, no matter how highly we have valued and cherished it during our life, can help. If we think of all our various possessions, our money, home or car, we can realize that when death comes none of these can prevent it. At the time of death seeking help from our possessions is futile: we have to leave everything behind when we depart from this life.

The second reason that Dharma alone can help us at the time of death is because our friends and relatives cannot aid us then. No matter how close we are to our friends and relatives or to our husband or wife, they cannot assist us when we have to die. At the time of death we have to depart from this life alone.

The third reason is that even our body which came from our mother's womb cannot help us at the time of death. Throughout our life we have protected and cherished our body. But this body cannot prevent our death, and when we die we will have to leave it behind.

Thus, at the time of death neither our possessions, friends, nor our own body can help. What can aid us at that time? Only Dharma can help. If, through the force of meditation and practising Dharma, we have achieved some spiritual realizations, these will help us. If we have gained some experience of Dharma and have received some meaning from our life, this will assist us at the time of death and in our future lives.

By thinking deeply about these three reasons why only Dharma can help us at the time of death, we should make a determination. We should decide to practise Dharma purely and think:

'During this short life I will practise only Dharma.'

As has been explained, the meditation on death and impermanence has three roots, nine reasons and three determinations. Making these three determinations fully is the fruit of the meditation and the sign that we have received the experience. Until we have fully made these three determinations, we should practise this meditation on impermanence. We should reflect on the impermanence teachings daily and constantly try to remind ourself that death is inevitable. No matter how effective modern medicine or how qualified our doctors, there is no cure for old age and death.

When we contemplate impermanence in this way we will begin to develop an intuitive feeling for the impermanence which pervades our life. Since death is definite and the time of our death is uncertain, it is foolish to think that we have no need to practise Dharma today. If we put off practising Dharma until tomorrow or the next day, by then it may be too late.

A summary of the three roots, nine reasons and three determinations is given below:

1 First root – Death is definite

Three reasons:

- I The process of death cannot be avoided
- II Our life span decreases with each passing moment and cannot be extended
- III Death is definite even if we have no time to practise Dharma

First determination: To practise Dharma

2 Second root — The time of death is indefinite

Three reasons:
- I Our life span is unfixed
- II Many conditions can lead to death and few sustain life
- III Our body is very delicate

Second determination: To practise Dharma right now

3 Third root — At the time of death only Dharma can help

Three reasons:
- I Our wealth and possessions cannot help us
- II Our friends and relatives cannot help us
- III Our body cannot help us

Third determination: To practise only Dharma

SUBTLE IMPERMANENCE

All examples of gross impermanence such as death develop from subtle impermanence. Knowing this is very important. Subtle impermanence is much more difficult to understand than gross impermanence; nevertheless, if we think deeply and precisely about subtle impermanence, we can begin to understand it. Subtle impermanence refers to the subtle changes which are constantly taking place within functioning things.

If we consider a watch, we can easily see that the second hand of the watch moves or changes very quickly. However, usually we are not aware that our own body, house, etc. are also changing with each passing second. But actually all things are changing every moment.

By observing carefully and precisely, we can realize that our body and possessions have subtle changes going on within them. This is subtle impermanence.

Chapter 4

REINCARNATION

If someone is a true Buddhist, he or she believes in rebirth or reincarnation. Owing to hearing and studying Buddhist teachings, and practising Dharma, some people can understand reincarnation by means of their own experience. Nevertheless, others, including some non-Buddhist philosophical schools, do not accept the existence of reincarnation.

There is a philosophical school called the *Charvakas* which does not believe in rebirth. When this school was asked,

'Why is there no rebirth?'

they had no perfect or correct answer. They said that reincarnation does not exist because any phenomenon which exists must be visible. Thus, they disbelieve rebirth because they cannot see it with their own eyes. This school believes only in manifested objects, not in hidden or extremely hidden objects.

Besides the school mentioned above, there are many people who deny rebirth. The main reason for this is that they have not seen reincarnation directly. But this is incorrect: it is very important to know about former lives and future lives. If we ignore former lives and future lives, then we hold wrong views such as denying rebirth. According to Buddhism, whoever believes there is no rebirth is holding a wrong view. Such a distorted view develops through the force of not knowing of the existence of past and future lives.

Nowadays people commonly believe in some hidden things such as tiny atoms or distant stars which they cannot see. By means of logical reasoning and other scientific evidence, they can know that these things exist. In the same way, we can know about rebirth even if we cannot see it.

There are two methods for understanding reincarnation. The first is the method which causes us to believe in a former or previous life. The second method causes us to believe in the next or future life. The explanation here will concentrate on the first method. If we know that there was a former life, then it is very easy to understand that there will be a future life. Altogether there are five techniques for understanding that we have had a previous life. The first technique is that through mental instincts or imprints we can know that there has been a former life. The second technique involves understanding the continuum of our mind. The third technique uses the force of dream appearances to show that there has been a former life. Fourth, through the force of examples we can know of a former life. The fifth technique is that through the force of scriptural authority we can know we have experienced a previous life.

If we meditate on these five techniques continuously, it is not very difficult to understand that there has been a former life. If we have a proper and discerning attitude, in general it is easy to understand former and future lives. If our attitude or motivation is wrong, then not even Christ or Buddha could make us believe in reincarnation. Even if a living Buddha explained reincarnation it would be very difficult to understand. But if, with the correct motivation and attitude, we think deeply about these five techniques, rebirth will be fairly easy to understand.

However, wrong discernment may interfere with one's understanding. For example, if a person is addicted to drugs and one of his friends advises against using drugs, he will not like the advice. That person has mistaken discernment. If someone has a wrong or distorted attitude like this, then it is difficult to understand rebirth.

1 MENTAL IMPRINTS

Even though we are all human beings, there is a wide variation in mental imprints and tendencies among people. Some people have very positive or wholesome mental imprints whereas others have many negative mental imprints. Everyone's mental imprints and tendencies are not the same.

Two children from the same family, for instance, can have totally different mental tendencies. The first child may have strong negative tendencies such as wishing to harm others, getting angry easily, and disliking wholesome actions. But the second child may have a good heart and the wish to help others and to perform positive actions. His intentions are beneficial. What, then, is the reason why parents can have children with such different types of minds? If we consider deeply, these mental tendencies are due to the experiences of previous lives. One child's mind is positive because he has accumulated positive imprints; the other child has accumulated negative imprints from negative thoughts and actions in past lives.

Adults, too, have different minds and mental imprints. Some adults hate religion as if it were a poison. But when others hear religious or Dharma teachings they regard them as a beneficial medicine. What is the cause of these two different ways of thinking? A person who instinctively dislikes religion disliked religion in previous lives. But a person who instinctively likes religion has the imprints of a wholesome regard for religion in former lives.

As another example, some people can learn a new language very quickly and easily. Other people find it extremely difficult to learn another language. This difference is due to their past lives' imprints.

The effects of mental imprints or tendencies can also be observed among Buddhists. Some Buddhists, despite energetic effort, have great difficulty in achieving spiritual realizations. But other Buddhists reach spiritual realizations easily, without making a great deal of effort. Therefore, spiritual realizations can be seen to be the fruit not only of this life's efforts, but also of past lives' efforts and tendencies. If we think about our own mental tendencies and imprints, then we can understand the existence of previous lives.

Visible examples of previous lives are difficult to find. But just as the smoke billowing from behind a mountain tells us that there has been a fire, likewise the effects of the mental imprints of our previous lives show us that there have been former lives.

2 THE CONTINUUM OF MIND

All external things have two causes. A clay pot, for example, has both a substantial cause and a contributing cause. The substantial cause is the clay which forms the pot. But along with the substantial cause, the contributing cause of the potter, the potter's actions, hands and tools is necessary. All external things need these two causes: the first or substantial cause, which is transformed into the nature of the product, and the contributing cause, which helps to transform the substantial cause into the product.

In the same way, all internal things such as mind have two causes:

substantial and contributing. The substantial cause of mind is the previous continuum of mind. The contributing cause of mind is meeting objects. That is, owing to the contact of our senses and objects, mind develops. In order to develop any kind of mind, these two causes – the previous continuum of mind and meeting an object – must be present.

The substantial cause of today's mind is yesterday's mind. Today's mind develops out of yesterday's mind. If we consider a baby, that baby's mind developed from the mind which was inside the mother's womb. The baby's consciousness first entered the mother's womb when the sperm and egg united. But that baby's mind came from its previous mind, from its previous life. By this method of tracing back the continuum of mind we can know that there has been a previous life.

3 DREAM APPEARANCES

Through the force of dream appearances we can understand the existence of a former life. In general, there are three types of dream appearances. The first type is the appearance of past happenings of this life. The second type of dream appearance indicates events which will be experienced later in this life. The third type of dream appearance relates to other lives, to former and future reincarnations.

The dream appearances of the early part of this life refer to dreams we have now about past events, for example about childhood. We can dream about past holidays, old homes, old friends, deceased relatives or parents. We can perceive all this now in the dreams about our early life.

Sometimes a dream appearance indicates something which will happen later in this life. We might dream that our parents are going to give us a present and the next day we find that our parents have sent us money. Our dreams are sometimes very true. We might dream of a place we have never visited and then several years later we do visit that place. Dreams can predict events which will occur later in this life.

Apart from these two types of dreams (about earlier and later parts of this life), any other dream appearance indicates either a future or former life's action. Sometimes one might dream of something which could not happen in this life. For instance, some ordinary beings might dream they could fly in the sky. If one frequently dreams about flying, this indicates the attainment of the concentration of tranquil abiding in a previous life or that one was in a past life a being able to fly.

A dream always indicates a former or future life if it does not relate to this present life. By checking our dream appearances it is easy to understand about past and future lives. Something we dream may seem impossible in terms of our present life, but it may occur in a future life or already have happened in a past life. Without any causes or conditions such dream appearances would not arise.

4 THE FORCE OF EXAMPLES

Some non-Buddhists maintain that reincarnation does not occur because there are no examples of rebirth. They may not have encountered people who can remember their past lives, but such people do exist. We cannot conclude that something does not exist just because certain people have not observed it. In fact, there are many instances of people who recall their previous lives. Two examples will be presented here.

In southern India a boy was born into a trading family. The boy's first words were,

'Where is my master?'

His mother, greatly surprised, asked,

'Who is your master?'

The child replied that his teacher or master was Vasubandhu. The following day the boy said that he wanted to see his teacher, who was in Magadha, in another part of India.

The boy's parents asked some traders about the Buddhist master their son had mentioned. The traders informed them that there was a highly realized teacher named Vasubandhu in Magadha. After receiving this information, the parents took the boy to Magadha to see Vasubandhu.

When they reached Magadha the parents asked Vasubandhu about the nature of his relationship with their child. Vasubandhu told them that when he was living in a cave in the mountains reciting the scriptures, there was a pigeon in his cave. The pigeon used to hear the scriptures Vasubandhu recited every day. The pigeon later died and through the force of hearing the Buddha's scriptures the bird's negativities were purified and he was reborn in human form as their son.

As he grew up the child learned everything he was taught very easily.

From his past life he had a strong karmic link with Vasubandhu. He became a highly realized yogi called Stirmati. This is a true story showing a former life.

There is a more recent example of rebirth which happened in this generation. When I was small I had a very wise teacher named Kachen Pella who lived in the western part of Tibet. Kachen Pella had many disciples. When he knew he was going to die, he distributed his books to his disciples.

Shortly before his death a woman from a town a thousand miles away came to where the teacher was living. The old teacher spoke to the woman whom he had never seen before and invited her to have tea with him. Before the woman left, the teacher gave her a white scarf and said,

'I will come to your house.* At that time please treat me well.'

The woman asked if the teacher knew her house. He replied,

'I will know your house.'

The woman thought that the old teacher wanted to make a pilgrimage, so she said he would be welcome to come to her house. Then she left and ten days later the teacher died at the time and on the date he had foretold. Those who had faith in the teacher believed he had foretold his death by clairvoyance; those without faith believed he had foretold it through astrology.

Not long after the teacher's death, the woman who had visited him had a baby. Her child began to speak about his previous life, about his monastery and the names of his disciples. The mother then learned that the old teacher had died and thought inwardly that her son might be the old teacher who had said he would come to her house. Although his mother said nothing, finally the news of the boy speaking about his previous life reached the old teacher's monastery and his disciples. A delegation of monks visited the child to see if he was the reincarnation of their teacher. When they arrived the boy called two monks by name and selected the rosary of his previous life from among six similar rosaries. The monks were convinced that this was the reincarnation of their guru.

The monks asked the mother if they could take the boy to their monastery where they would care for him well. The mother said that she had no doubts that the child was indeed the reincarnation of their

*The Tibetan custom of giving a white scarf is a sign of auspiciousness.

teacher, but because he was her only son she would not allow him to go to the monastery.

After two years the boy became very ill and was about to die. His mother consulted the local lama about his illness. The lama advised her to let the boy go to the monastery, otherwise he would die. Not wishing her son to die, she sent him to the monastery.

The boy became a monk and was given the name of Kachen Pella, the same name as the old teacher. I was one of his disciples and there are many more of his disciples still living in India who can verify that this is a true story. The reincarnation of this teacher is now about thirty years old and is living in Tibet.

Tibetans do not believe all the claims of children who say they recall their past lives. They investigate these claims carefully before deciding if they are true. They set up an examination body to test whether someone remembers his past life correctly. The living realized beings who remember their former lives are true examples of the fact that there are past and future lives.

Furthermore, many people in the West as well as in the East can recall their previous life. Many children can remember some details of a past life such as their parents' names. These too are true examples of a past life. If we examine these examples carefully, there is no doubt that reincarnation occurs.

5 SCRIPTURAL AUTHORITY

Relying on scriptural authority to demonstrate rebirth depends upon one's faith in the scriptures, the words of the Buddha. For non-Buddhists, the Buddha's statements about reincarnation may not be sufficient to dispel doubts. But a Buddhist who has strong faith in the Buddha will be convinced by what he said about rebirth.

There are many scriptures in which the Buddha explained that there is rebirth. In one Sutra the Buddha said:

> 'In one of my previous lives I was punished by the king of Kalinga. He had my limbs chopped off, but even at that time I had no self-grasping, no attachment and no anger.'

Thus, we can see that the Buddha had already become a very highly realized being in a previous life. In this Sutra it is clearly shown by Buddha that there has been a former life.

There is a biography describing 108 former lives of the Buddha. This biography is based on the scriptural authority of the Buddha. If we have faith, we can know from scriptural authority that there is rebirth. If we have no faith, then we can use logical reasoning to prove that there is reincarnation. If we use the five techniques explained here it is not difficult to understand reincarnation. Once we know that there was a previous life, it follows logically that there will be a future life.

Eventually our body will decay and die, but our mind never dies. After death our body can be burnt, but this is not the case with our mind. Mind and body are totally different. At death or sometimes even before death, the mind leaves the body.

Highly realized meditators can cause their minds to leave their bodies and enter other bodies. Marpa's son, a Bodhisattva or being who was seeking full Enlightenment in order to benefit others, was able to perform this transference of mind. After his body was seriously injured in a riding accident, Marpa's son decided to seek a new body into which he could transfer his mind. For this purpose he needed a flawless corpse. He could not find a human body immediately, but he found the corpse of a pigeon. Marpa's son transferred his mind into the pigeon's body and the pigeon's form was restored to life. With the form of a bird, Marpa's son could not do much to help others; therefore he continued to search for a human body in order to fulfil his wish to benefit sentient beings.

Through the force of his father's clairvoyance, Marpa's son eventually found in India the corpse of a realized yogi. The mind of Marpa's son left the pigeon and entered the yogi's body. With this human body Marpa's son lived for many years in India, giving Dharma teachings. Some people came even from Tibet to receive teachings from him.

According to Tibetan Buddhism there are many techniques for causing the mind to enter into another body. This practice flourished for a time. If the mind can leave the body in this way before death, then of course at the time of death the mind leaves the body and does not die. There is something more after this life. By studying these five techniques we can know that there is a life to come after this one.

In general, Buddhists regard future lives as being more important than this present life. That is, whatever sufferings or adverse conditions we encounter in our present life, we should not become discouraged. Instead we should realize that we now have the opportunity to practise Dharma, to improve our mind by eliminating negative actions and practising virtue. Thus, we can create the conditions now for higher rebirths, for practising Dharma in future lives and for the final attainment of full Enlightenment.

Chapter 5

ACTIONS AND THEIR EFFECTS

Wholesome actions bring only happiness and never suffering. From the greatest king to the most insignificant animal, all the happiness sentient beings know is the result of their wholesome actions. Buddhists believe that if someone has a pleasant or happy life now, this is because of positive actions he or she committed in past lives. It is also possible that virtuous actions performed earlier in our present life will produce positive results later in the same lifetime. According to Buddhism, our physical and mental well-being and happiness result from our own accumulated positive actions or positive karma. Thus, the cause of happiness is wholesome karma.

Followers of the non-Buddhist *Charvaka* school of philosophy hold the view that there is no cause which produces happiness. They believe that all functioning things, including the roundness of peas, the sharpness of thorns, and the 'eyes' on peacocks' feathers, occur without causes. This philosophical school believes that these types of physical things are not produced by causes. Therefore they conclude that all phenomena – even happiness and misery – arise without any cause. This view is rejected by all Buddhist schools.

Buddhists believe that without causes there cannot be any results. When a seed has been sown a sprout will emerge in a few days or weeks. Sprouts are produced from causes, from seeds. In the same way that sprouts arise from seeds, all other functioning things also arise from causes. Just as external things such as sprouts depend upon causes, likewise internal things, such as mind, also depend on causes. There is no thing which does not have a cause.

Another non-Buddhist school, the *Samkyas*, maintain that happiness is produced by a primal substance or general principle. Their concept of a primal substance is similar to a concept of god. They believe that happiness and misery are derived from the primal substance. The Buddhist schools of philosophy do not accept this view. Positing the existence of a primal substance does not explain how dissatisfaction and suffering arise.

The non-Buddhist *Vaisheshikas* assert that both happiness and suffering are caused by gods such as Ishvara. According to this view, the external environment as well as happiness and misery are caused by gods. Buddhists consider that this view is incorrect. The Buddhist view is that whoever has a happy or peaceful mind has created this through his or her own actions, and equally, whoever has an unhappy mind and much suffering has produced this by his or her actions or karma. Thus, happiness and misery are not caused by gods like Ishvara, but by individuals themselves.

Our happiness was not given to us by Ishvara because he does not have the power to grant happiness to all sentient beings without exception. If Ishvara did have the power to bestow happiness on all transmigrating beings, why would he inflict suffering on them instead? Especially since all sentient beings wish for happiness and not suffering, what would Ishvara's purpose be in inflicting suffering on sentient beings? If we consider this carefully, we will understand that happiness and suffering depend on karma, not on a god.

According to Buddhism, all happiness derives from positive causes and conditions, from our wholesome actions of body, speech and mind. All the different forms of anxiety, dissatisfaction and suffering result from our negative karma — our negative actions of body, speech and mind. This becomes clear through analogy with an external example of causation.

A poisonous seed will produce a poisonous plant, but a medicinal seed will only grow into a medicinal plant. A pea seed will produce peas, not wheat; and a wheat seed will yield wheat and never peas. Whatever is the nature of the cause, its effect will be of the same nature. Negative causes create negative effects while positive causes produce positive ones.

If we wish to experience impeccable happiness, we should strive to produce extremely positive karma. If we create negative karma, the result will be unbearable suffering. It is very important to think about karma and its functions. Until we fully understand karma we should investigate how it operates — how good actions lead to good results and bad actions lead to bad results. The powerful conviction that good fruit derives from good causes and bad fruit derives from bad causes is the real foundation for all Buddhist teachings and for all virtuous practices. If we are not convinced about karma it is very difficult to practise Dharma purely.

Not believing that good causes produce good results is a wrong view and this thought is an obstacle to practising Dharma. It closes the door to liberation. If we try to understand positive and negative karma and try to abandon negative actions and practise virtuous actions, our life will become meaningful. Whoever does not wish to experience suffering should try to abandon negative actions; whoever wishes to experience happiness should practise wholesome actions.

Up to the present we have experienced many problems because of having created negative causes. What we have to do from now on is to perform positive actions of body, speech and mind so that our behaviour will become pure and clean. If we do this, then in future there will be no basis from which problems and difficulties will arise. Believing in ripening karma, that is, believing that good causes bring about good results and bad causes bring about bad results, is a particularly beneficial practice for worldly people. By teaching people such a view as this, Dharma helps groups and societies as well as individuals. If we hold this view of ripening karma, we will have fewer problems and we will not waste our life in meaningless pursuits.

THE IMPORTANCE OF SMALL ACTIONS

Some actions, even though they are small, can create a great amount of happiness or misery. Even a tiny action can cause enormous results, just as a tiny seed can become a huge tree. Some small negative actions can bring much suffering and some small positive actions can lead to great happiness. Therefore, we should not overlook even the smallest action as we try to abandon negative karma and create positive karma. We should never think that a negative action is so small that it does not matter. Rather, we should realize that it is essential to eliminate even the tiniest negative karma because it can bring immense suffering.

A little poison ingested can cause death or dangerous illness. Can we say that it is only a little poison? It can do no harm and does not matter? If we think in this way and take poison, we may well die. The same is true for even the tiniest negative karma: it can lead to incredible suffering. Therefore we should work to eliminate even the smallest negative karma, regarding it as if it were deadly poison.

When we perform small positive actions we should not regard them as insignificant or hesitate to practise them because they seem unimportant. They can result in great happiness. The mango seed is small, but the mango tree is huge and its fruits are numerous. In the same manner, small wholesome actions can produce enormous positive results for us.

Beings wish to experience many different kinds of happiness, both physical and mental. Happiness is derived from wholesome or positive karma. For example, having a beautiful or attractive physical body is mainly the result of having practised patience. The happiness which results from having wealth is caused by positive karma, specifically by the practice of generosity in the past.

Compared to animals, humans have special happiness because of their human form. The happiness of being human is the result of good karma. The cause of this good karma is having kept moral discipline. Each kind of happiness has a different positive cause. These kinds of karma are quite easy to understand. It is easy to understand that being wealthy is the result of practising generosity because the cause and its effect resemble each other.

THE INSEPARABILITY OF KARMA AND THE MIND

There are two kinds of karma: negative and positive. We create our own karma — whether negative or positive — and this karma is inseparable from us. Our body and its shadow never separate; wherever the body goes, the shadow goes too. There is no way to take the body and leave the shadow behind. Likewise, we are never separated from the karma we create, no matter whether it is virtuous or non-virtuous. When we go on to our next life it is impossible to leave our negative and positive karma behind. Wherever we take rebirth, our karma will be there too.

We may become separated from our home or friends in this life, but we can never be separated from the karma we have created. If our positive karma is greater than our negative karma, then wherever we will be reborn we will have a joyful life with one pleasure after another. Our present life as well as our future lives will be pleasant. But if we have a greater store of negative karma, our present life will be unhappy and our future lives will also be full of misery.

A tourist who has a great deal of money can travel around the world without problems; he can go wherever he wishes to seek enjoyment. But someone who goes to a distant country without any money will have many difficulties and will not find pleasure there. Likewise, someone who has much virtuous karma will encounter favourable circumstances, but a person without this stock of merit or positive karma will encounter numerous problems. Thus, if we wish to have a good life we should discriminate between negative and positive karma, striving to abandon the former and accumulate the latter.

JUDGING OUR KARMA

In our daily activities we should judge whether we are creating more negative or positive karma. Usually we calculate our money very carefully, but a pure Dharma practitioner should be even more careful to assess his or her negative and positive karma. This is extremely important.

At the moment we ignore karma altogether. We do not know when we create negative karma or when we create positive karma. Our life ebbs away unheeded. We need to practise being mindful of the karma we produce — observing if the karma we create is more often non-virtuous or virtuous.

If we discover that we have created more positive karma we can congratulate ourself. On the other hand, if we have created more negative karma we should make a confession. Practising sincerely like this, our activities will gradually become purer. We should follow the example of Geshe Ben Gungyel.

Before he became a monk Geshe Ben Gungyel was a bandit robbing travellers and stealing from houses at night. He committed many negative actions. Finally he met a guru who gave him teachings on Dharma and he felt great regret about his previous negative actions and confessed them. He then became a monk.

But even as a monk his ingrained habit of stealing caused him problems. One day he was invited to the home of a benefactor and was left sitting alone in the shrine room for a few moments. He noticed a block of tea lying on top of a sack. He reached out his hand to steal the tea, but then he remembered he was a monk and that he was about to do something wrong. He experienced great remorse and called his benefactor:

> 'Come here and look at this hand! See what this thief is doing! Cut off my right hand now. I am so used to stealing that I cannot stop even now that I am a monk.'

From that moment on Geshe Ben Gungyel observed his actions very carefully and behaved impeccably. From the first thing in the morning until the last thing at night he judged his actions, trying to eliminate negative actions and practise wholesome ones. He added up his positive and negative karma daily by putting white and black stones on his table. For a positive action he put a white stone on his table, while for a negative action of body, speech or mind he put out a black stone. If, at the end of the day, he found more black stones than white he criticized himself, shaking his left hand with his right and saying,

> 'You robber, don't you have to die? Do you have any choice in your next rebirth? Do you have any freedom at all when you commit so many bad actions?'

He would be disgusted with himself and confess his negative actions to all the Buddhas.

However, if Geshe Ben Gungyel discovered more white stones than black on his table at the end of the day, he would shake his own right hand with his left and praise himself,

> 'You have done very well.'

He would congratulate himself on his positive actions and call himself 'Venerable Geshe'. In this way he appreciated his wholesome actions and encouraged himself in practising them. He spent his life like this. The great Indian master Padampa Sangye praised Geshe Ben Gungyel's spiritual practices highly. He said that serious Dharma practitioners should follow the Geshe's example, trying to eliminate negative actions and cultivating positive ones.

Most people look at the faults of others and criticize them, but there is no value in doing this. Instead of criticizing others, we should discover our own faults and try to remove them. If we cannot recognize our faults through mindfulness it will be very difficult to accept the criticisms of others; these will only produce anger. If we do not discover our faults or learn of them through the remarks of others, we will continue to perform negative actions until death. Shakyamuni Buddha said that a person who looks for faults in others is not wise or skilful. But a person who looks for his or her own faults is skilful. He who judges himself and his own mistakes is truly wise. As Atisha said, we should judge our own faults and not the faults of others. Whenever we commit negative actions we should drop them as we would drop hot iron.

We should not think of our own knowledge and qualifications as this causes arrogance to arise. Instead, we should think of the knowledge and qualifications of others; we should respect and venerate others. The results of our actions are similar to their causes. Thus, by respecting others we will naturally be respected ourself. If we respect others without envy and jealousy, then we too will be respected in this way. However, if we are highly critical of others, people will begin to show disrespect to us. This is very beneficial advice.

In one Sutra the Buddha explained that one may be rich, powerful, attractive, and born into a high caste. But if one does not practise generosity, morality, patience and other wholesome actions, but instead practises non-virtuous actions, one's situation will become poor, even terrifying in future lives. Yet in this life one had near-perfect conditions. In contrast, if one is poor, of low rank, unattractive and powerless, but practises virtue in this life, then one will attain happiness in future lives.

INANIMATE OBJECTS CANNOT CREATE KARMA

If we do not commit wholesome or unwholesome actions we will not receive the fruit of happiness or unhappiness. Inanimate objects such as stones, water, fire and trees do not experience happiness or suffering. They have no ability to produce karma; and happiness and suffering depend solely upon karma. Karma cannot ripen on inanimate objects, but only on sentient beings. Only beings with a mind create karma.

To produce positive karma we must have the correct motivation. Since the production of karma depends on motivation, mindless phenomena do not have the ability to create karma. Some people believe that flowers and plants have minds because they can move or respond to stimuli such as light. For example, if we pour water on to a wilting flower it straightens up. However, this movement is due not to mind, but to the action of internal energy winds.

Some of the *Nirgranthas*, members of a non-Buddhist school of philosophy, argued that plants do have minds because they die if someone damages them. This is an imperfect reason: if something has a mind, that mind must have an object. Without meeting an object, consciousness can never arise. A mind must have something to cognize. Plants have no consciousnesses which can arise to meet objects. Thus, plants do not satisfy the criteria for having mind.

ACTIONS WILL NOT BE FRUITLESS

In the same way that if we do not sow the seeds we cannot harvest the crops, if we do not create wholesome karma we cannot experience happiness. Likewise, if we do not produce unwholesome karma we cannot experience suffering. But once karma has been created, its result will never be lost. External things decay and become useless with age, but karma is not like that. Karma does not decay and cannot be destroyed by time, fire or water. Its potential power will never disappear until it has ripened. Karmic imprints from actions we performed many aeons ago are still upon our consciousness. The mind is like a storehouse of karma, holding many different kinds of karma produced in past lives.

We have countless negative and positive karmas and each has a different function. All these karmas are like seeds and our mind at the time of death is like water. Any karma meeting the right conditions will ripen. Just as there are many seeds in the ground but only those which are watered will grow, only karmas which meet the right conditions will ripen.

At the time of death, if we pray to obtain a human rebirth this is a wholesome mind. This mind is like water and the moral discipline we have kept in this life or in past lives is like the seed. When the seed of moral discipline and the water of prayer meet we will obtain a human rebirth. For rebirth as a Deva or god it is the same: at the time of death moral discipline and prayer meet. The fervent prayer,

> 'How wonderful if I was reborn as a Deva,'

is a wholesome prayer. It is like water and when it meets the seed of moral discipline it will ripen into a Deva rebirth. By this process karma ripens.

Karma – whether wholesome or unwholesome – never disappears until its result ripens. But the purification of accumulated negative karma is possible. Only declaration or confession of non-virtuous actions can dispel the potential power of negative karma.

The principal cause of the destruction of wholesome karma is anger or hatred. The main function of anger is to destroy virtuous karma.

Unless destroyed by anger, the seeds of wholesome karma will not disappear until they ripen, and the result of the wholesome karma will be happiness. The result of karma is fixed: positive karma brings happiness and negative karma brings suffering.

The potential power of karma will not be reduced. For this reason the accumulated karma of migrating beings is extremely powerful and dynamic. When our karma is ripening, not even a Buddha can prevent the result.

CHAPTER 6

WHAT IS MIND?

Unless we reach liberation, it is an inescapable condition of human existence to suffer from dissatisfaction. Expecting solutions to our problems to come from outside ourself, or looking to others for solutions can prevent us from trying to make progress. There are techniques and methods available for dealing with problems. As it is our own responsibility to overcome our problems, we must search for, investigate and use the methods for dealing with our difficulties.

One of the best methods for dealing with problems is to gain control of our own mind. Mind transformation is a powerful method for solving problems. This is because all human dissatisfaction and misery arises from the mind and depends upon it. What feels the effects of troubles and miseries? It is the mind because these feelings are a part of the mind. Stones, for example, unlike humans have no feelings because they have no minds.

Problems and dissatisfaction do not develop because of external conditions, but from our own mind. No matter how many external conditions conducive to happiness we have, if we have no internal peace, no amount of wealth or possessions can bring us happiness. But a person who has nothing — no house or possessions — can be happy if he or she has peace of mind.

It is our mind which has created the actions which cause us to experience suffering and to be born into cyclic existence or samsara. The only way to reach Buddhahood is by training in the control and transformation of our mind, until finally we can free our mind completely from all defilements and obscurations.

Without good motivation it is impossible to perform positive actions. Intentions always precede our actions. Thus, the root of our good and bad actions is our mind. All our physical, verbal and mental actions depend on our mind.

How things appear to us depends on our mind. It is through our perceptions that we know that phenomena exist. If our mind could not perceive anything, we would not be able to know whether anything exists.

In general, everyone believes in the existence of mind, but very few people understand its precise nature. The Buddha and many yogis and yoginis have studied the mind closely. It is the results of these studies and my own experiences which will now be explained.

Mind is defined as clarity and knowing. Clarity is the nature of the mind. Mind is also formless. We all have a mind whose essential nature is clear and unobscured by any defilement. Just as the clouds which obscure the sky are transient and not inextricably mixed with the nature of the sky, likewise the delusions and defilements which obscure our mind are not permanent. Delusions and misconceptions are temporary phenomena which are not mixed with the pure nature of the mind.

Knowing is the function of the mind. The mind perceives, apprehends and knows its object. It discerns and discriminates between forms, qualities, aspects and so forth. The mind studies and learns. The operations of the mind are very extensive.

Objects of knowledge can be divided into permanent and impermanent objects. Mind is an impermanent object of knowledge because it changes with every passing moment.

THE LOCATION OF THE MIND

It is pointless to search for our mind outside our body. Equally, our body and mind are not the same. Different philosophical schools have different ideas about the location of the mind. Some say it is at the heart, some say the brain, and others say that it pervades the entire body. Many experienced and realized meditators say that mind exists throughout the whole body.

The body is pervaded by the body faculty, i.e. the potential for the development of body consciousness. For example, if something touches our hand, body consciousness develops. This is because when our hand is touched feeling arises and this feeling is mind. The same applies for all other parts of the body. Thus, mind pervades all parts of our body.

Our secondary minds include all of the feelings which develop in the different parts of the body. All the different types of secondary minds arise from the one root mind which is located at our heart. Within the brain there is mind, but the brain itself is not the mind. By contemplating upon the different aspects of mind — its nature, location and divisions — we can begin to develop a mental image or concept of the mind. If we meditate on the mind it is very beneficial to visualize it at our heart, although this may be difficult for some people.*

MEDITATION ON THE MIND

There are many different objects for meditation. These fall into two categories: internal and external. An example of an external object of meditation is visualizing the Buddha in front of us. Our mind is an internal object of meditation. Meditation is like medicine which can cure all of our delusions and bring us to have a calm and peaceful mind.

Meditation can be divided into two types: analytical and placement. In analytical meditation, by contemplation and investigation, recalling what we know about the mind and exploring it, we discover the mind gradually and can build up a concept of it. This concept is then used as the object of our placement meditation.

At present our conception of our mind is not clear, but only a rough idea. Through continuous meditation we can gradually perceive our mind clearly and purely. First we should try to overcome mental wandering and abandon conceptual distractions. We should focus our mind within and observe whatever arises: thoughts, sensations of body, hearing, smelling, tasting and images. Consider how these arise, where they come from and where they go. Consider what is the nature of the mind. Recalling the teachings will help.

Recognizing the nature of the mind, we should concentrate on this and hold this recognition as clearly as possible. This placement meditation can reduce defilements and is a very good way to achieve tranquil abiding. It can also reduce anger and attachment. Problems of an over-busy mind, distractions and so forth are overcome by concentrating on the mind and holding this calmness as long as possible. Altogether this meditation is very beneficial and can transform our mind and make it more wholesome.

This is the first stage of Dharma practice: to overcome personal problems and negative thoughts and to achieve calmness and control. One should listen, study and meditate, and thus understand, change and solve one's problems. The second stage — to be entered upon only

*Here 'heart' means the centre of the chest just in front of the spine.

when one has gained the experience of the first stage — is to try to guide others.

It is important to know the complete spiritual path in order not to go off in the wrong direction at any stage. Intellectual understanding alone is insufficient for this. But through intellectual understanding together with experience, our Dharma practice will become stronger month by month and year by year.

DIVISIONS OF THE MIND

There is only one root mind, but there are many other types of mind which arise from the root mind. Countless different kinds of conceptual thoughts exist, all of which are mind. These thoughts fall into three categories: wholesome minds, unwholesome minds, and neutral or indifferent minds.

Wholesome minds

Wholesome minds include compassion, faith, generosity, love, patience, wishing to help others, and so forth. Wholesome thoughts such as these create peace of mind.

Wholesome minds can be used to dispel negative minds. Meditation on love can be used to dispel anger. Meditation on appreciation and rejoicing in the good qualities of others can be used to overcome the problem of jealousy. Meditation on impermanence and death awareness counteracts covetousness. Meditating on an object's repulsiveness reduces attachment. Meditation on emptiness can eradicate completely all the aforementioned negative thoughts. By practising these wholesome meditations we can arrive at inner peace. The purpose of Dharma is to solve our inner problems and to develop peace of mind.

Unwholesome minds

Negative or unwholesome minds are the cause of our suffering, confusion and misery. Aggression, anger, hatred, harmful thoughts, wrong views, ignorance, jealousy, etc. are all unwholesome minds. From our own experience we can see how these minds are harmful to us and destroy our inner peace and tranquillity. Self-grasping is the root of all these harmful minds.

Neutral minds

Neutral minds are neither wholesome nor unwholesome. But like a white cloth which can be dyed different colours, neutral minds can transform into positive or negative minds. The minds which develop during sleep, for example, are largely neutral although sometimes we may develop wholesome or unwholesome minds during sleep. In our waking hours we also experience many examples of neutral minds. Wishing to go from one place to another or wishing to sit down are instances of neutral or indifferent minds.

All of our many conceptions fall within these three categories. We should check our conceptual thoughts every day to see into which categories they fall.

Conceptual and non-conceptual minds

In addition to the divisions mentioned above, minds can be divided into conceptions and non-conceptions. All minds are either conceptual or non-conceptual. The five sense consciousnesses are non-conceptual while the mental consciousness can be either conceptual or non-conceptual. Non-conceptual thought is defined as the mental process which perceives or apprehends its object directly or intuitively. It perceives its object very clearly. By contrast, conceptual thought perceives its object indirectly and unclearly through a generic image.

For example, when we see our mother, using our eye consciousness we perceive her clearly and directly. Therefore, this eye consciousness is non-conceptual mind. If we then close our eyes and try to remember our mother, we cannot perceive her clearly. We can still understand what she looks like, her size and shape, but the appearance is not very clear. Thus, at this time the mind which recollected our mother is conceptual. This example can be applied in a similar way to the recollection of other objects.

As another example, when we first hear teachings about impermanence we can understand them in a rough way. But our understanding is not very clear. At this time our mind which perceives impermanence is a conceptual mind. Subsequently, if we meditate continuously on impermanence, our appearance of impermanence will become clearer and clearer and we will eventually realize impermanence directly. This mind which realizes impermanence directly is non-conceptual. This example is true not only for impermanence, but also for all other hidden phenomena such as emptiness.

It is very helpful to know the difference between conceptual and non-conceptual minds. We all have these two types of minds, even if we do not recognize them. We should investigate how many conceptual and how many non-conceptual minds arise during the course of the day. By doing this we gain an expert understanding of our mind. Buddhahood, the fully awakened state of mind, is achieved by developing and improving our mind. Therefore it is essential to understand the different types of minds.

CHAPTER 7

THE DEVELOPMENT OF THE SIX CONSCIOUSNESSES

The nature of the primary mind and the nature of its secondary minds are identical, but the functions of these minds are different, like one family whose members do different things. The primary mind perceives the nature of the object and apprehends its general aspect. For example, with his primary mind a man perceives his watch as a whole. The secondary minds apprehend the characteristics of the object. With his secondary minds the man perceives in more detail the colour, size, shape, etc. of his watch.

The secondary minds perceive the many parts of which every object consists. The Buddhist master Asanga said that the mind which principally perceives the general aspect of an object is primary mind. The minds which principally perceive the parts of the object are secondary minds.

To examine the mind in this way is much more important than researching external things. This is because the root of our happiness is our own mind, not external phenomena. If our mind remains deluded, no matter how much outer success or development we may achieve, our problems and unhappiness will continue. Therefore, it is particularly important that we should observe and try to understand our own mind.

SIX KINDS OF CONSCIOUSNESS

Most people have all of the six consciousnesses or six primary minds described here. Just as there are six consciousnesses, there are six objects of consciousness. The six objects are: form, sound, smell, taste, touch, and any object not included in these five. In dependence upon meeting these objects, the six consciousnesses (the eye, ear, nose, tongue, body, and mental consciousnesses) develop. Thus, there are only six types of primary minds.

Some lower schools of Buddhism believe that there are eight consciousnesses, two more added to those mentioned above. This difference is due to the different views held by higher and lower schools of Buddhism. Different views were taught by the Buddha according to the level of intelligence of his listeners. Higher teachings or views were reserved for those of high intelligence, and lower teachings were given to those of lesser mental capacity.

1 Eye consciousness

Consciousness develops from its dominant condition. That is, the eye consciousness develops from the eye faculty. The eye faculty focuses on visual forms and the eye consciousness apprehends the forms.

The function of the eye consciousness is to perceive and apprehend visual forms. Without the eye consciousness we could not behold any visual form. But the eye consciousness itself depends on the eye faculty.

When the eye faculty and any form meet, the eye consciousness develops instantly. If the eye faculty and the form never meet, eye consciousness will never arise. In a permanently blind person the eye faculty is not present, and therefore the eye consciousness can never develop. Equally, if someone has this eye faculty but never encounters any visual form, no eye consciousness will ever arise.

The eye faculty is not the same as the eye consciousness. The eye faculty is a potential power that causes eye consciousness to develop immediately which is located within the physical eye. Our internal energy wind provides this power. During sleep we do not have this potential power or eye faculty because at that time our energy winds all gather inwards towards our heart and do not function outwardly.

If we know the nature of the eye faculty we can change it during this life. By means of meditation we can transform our eye faculty to achieve the divine eye, the eye with which we can see very distant things. Our physical eye remains the same, but the eye faculty is transformed. Only through meditation techniques can we change our eye faculty from a lower to a higher state in this way. Many yogis have achieved visual clairvoyance. Through meditation tranquil abiding can be achieved and the force of this tranquil abiding can be used to change the eye faculty.

However, miracle powers like clairvoyance and so forth are not very high spiritual realizations. The result of practising Dharma purely is the attainment of nirvana or Buddhahood, the attainment of true peace of mind and the ability to benefit others.

2 Ear consciousness

The other four sense consciousnesses are easy to understand through analogy to the eye consciousness. The nature of the ear faculty is not the physical ear. The ear faculty is a potential power that causes ear consciousness to develop immediately which is located within the physical ear. By transforming the ear faculty through meditation, one can develop auditory clairvoyance.

3 Nose consciousness

The nose consciousness develops immediately from the dominant condition of the nose faculty when it focuses on a smell. The nose faculty or the potential power to develop nose consciousness is not the same as the physical nose. Some people who have a physical nose structure nevertheless have no sense of smell. The nose faculty is a potential power that causes nose consciousness to develop immediately which is located within the physical nose. The nose faculty has to be present to enable the olfactory consciousness to develop and for smells to be apprehended.

4 Tongue consciousness

Tongue consciousness develops immediately through the dominant condition of the tongue faculty. When the tongue faculty focuses on a taste, the tongue consciousness develops. One then experiences, recognizes and distinguishes between tastes. The actual tongue faculty is a potential power located within the physical tongue.

Just before death the dying person cannot taste or smell; he or she cannot recognize close relatives. Already the energy winds of the sense organs are dissolving inwards. The functions of the sense consciousnesses fail as the energy winds diminish. The same process of dissolving the energy winds inwards also occurs during sleep and in deep meditation.

5 Body consciousness

Body or tactile consciousness develops when the dominant condition, the body faculty, meets an object of touch. The body faculty is a potential power which causes body consciousness to develop immediately. The location of the body faculty is throughout the entire body.

All of the five sense consciousnesses are temporary minds. Sometimes they are manifest, as when we see, hear, smell, taste or touch; and sometimes they are inactive.

6 Mental consciousness

The development of the first five consciousnesses depends on their five sense faculties and their five objects. The sixth consciousness is the mental consciousness. By analysing this explanation of the mental consciousness, we can discover if it is real or not. The mental consciousness is a mind which does not depend on any of the five sense faculties, but on the continuum of mind.

The first five consciousnesses are easy to recognize and understand. The mental consciousness is slightly more difficult to recognize. However, if we receive precise instructions about the mental consciousness, it is not difficult to understand. The definition of mental consciousness is a mind which does not depend on any of the five senses, but depends only on the immediately preceding continuum of mind.

We should use our own innate wisdom to examine all these things. Relying on what others say is not enough. It is necessary to listen to teachings, read books and consider these things for ourself, in the light of our experience. Buddha himself said that although he had shown all of the spiritual paths leading to Buddhahood, it was up to individuals to verify his teachings through their own experiences.

There are six consciousnesses, six objects of the consciousnesses, and six faculties. The object of the visual consciousness is only visual form. The object of the auditory consciousness is only sound. The object of the olfactory consciousness is only smell, whilst the object of the gustatory consciousness is only taste. In the same way, the object of the tactile consciousness is only the tangible object. The mental consciousness, however, has six objects including the objects of form, sound, taste, smell and touch, along with any other phenomena not included in these five objects.

The objects of the mental consciousness are more extensive than the objects of the senses. But how does a visual form become the object of the mental consciousness? For example, if we went shopping and saw some beautiful or attractive objects and then returned home and remembered those things, the mind which remembered the objects would be mental consciousness. The mental consciousness apprehends past visual forms. The visual consciousness perceives present visual forms, but all past visual forms are the objects of mental consciousness.

At first our visual consciousness perceives a visual form, then our mental consciousness cognizes the past visual form. If we meditate on the Buddha's form after seeing an image of the Buddha, it is our mental consciousness which visualizes that form. Sounds, too, can be the objects of our mental consciousness if we remember a sound which our hearing originally perceived. Likewise, tastes, smells, and sensations of touch can be the objects of our mental consciousness.

The mental consciousness is the most useful part of our mind. Not only can it cognize a wider range of objects than the five senses, it also performs other functions. It creates our daily plans, such as planning to study or perform daily chores. The root of all our actions is our mind. Before we perform an action our mind must prepare it. That is, if we have no mental wish to do something, we will not do it. Any action we do perform must be prepared by our mind. This is the case for both positive and negative actions: they arise from our beneficial or harmful mental intentions.

Our future happiness or misery depends upon our mind. If our mind prepares good actions, certainly we will receive good results in the future. In the same way, if our mind plans evil actions we will receive evil effects. According to Buddhism, this is the law of cause and effect or karma.

Because all the actions we create — whether positive or negative — depend on our mind, it is extremely important to judge the nature of our own mind. It is our responsibility to eliminate our negative actions and to cultivate positive actions. If we say that our actions depend on our mind, this means they depend on our mental consciousness. The first five consciousnesses only perceive objects; they cannot create our actions. Thus, it is mainly our mental consciousness which creates our actions.

There are many levels of mental consciousness, but in general these can be divided into three principal levels. The first level is gross mental consciousness. The next level is subtle mental consciousness and the third level is the very subtle mental consciousness. The first five consciousnesses do not have these different levels; they function only on the gross level. The first five consciousnesses are temporary minds. But the sixth or mental consciousness goes on from one life to the next.

One reason why Buddhists believe in reincarnation is because the continuous stream of mental consciousness passes on from this life to one's future life. When Buddhists demonstrate rebirth by means of the continuum of consciousness, it is not the gross mental consciousness to which they refer. It is the very subtle mental consciousness which continues from one life to another.

How can we distinguish between gross, subtle, and very subtle mental consciousness? In general, all the mental consciousness which functions during the daytime is gross mental consciousness. Likewise, any conceptual thought that arises during the daytime is gross mental consciousness. At the present time we are only able to use the gross mental consciousness, not the subtle and very subtle consciousnesses.

The subtle mental consciousness develops during sleep and also during the death process. Usually, a mind which develops during sleep is subtle. Dream minds are also subtle consciousnesses. Even though our consciousness during sleep is a subtle consciousness, there are many levels — some subtler and some more gross — within our mind of sleep.

Why is the mind we have during sleep called a subtle mind? The reason is that at present we cannot use this type of mind. If we think of something during the day, we can remember our thoughts, we can use our gross mind. But during sleep we cannot use our memory because at that time our consciousness is subtle.

In general, unless someone is an advanced meditator or realized being, it is difficult to use memory during sleep or in dreams. But if one has some acquaintance with Dharma and performs particular practices, it is possible to recognize certain things in one's sleep and dreams.

Eight signs

Eight levels of mind develop during the sleep process. Each level has a different sign. The first level's sign is the mirage-like appearance. Within the body are four elements: earth, water, fire and air. Accompanying each element is its energy wind. The mirage-like appearance develops when the energy wind of the earth element dissolves inwardly. But since at present we cannot use our recollection or mindfulness during sleep, we cannot recognize these signs or appearances precisely. But if we carefully study the nature of these signs, it becomes possible to recognize them.

When we develop the mind which perceives the mirage-like appearance, this is a relatively gross mind. Within the subtle mind of sleep, some minds are relatively more gross and some more subtle than others.

Next we perceive the second appearance, the smoke-like appearance. This appearance is perceived when the energy wind related to the water element dissolves inwardly. When the psychic or energy wind of the water element dissolves, we perceive the smoke-like appearance instantly. Within the mind of sleep, the mind which perceives the smoke-like appearance is subtler than the previous mind but is still a relatively gross mind.

After this we perceive the third sign, the fireflies-like appearance. This appearance arises when the energy wind which is related to our fire element dissolves inwardly. The fourth sign is the burning butter lamp-like appearance. It is perceived instantly when the energy wind of our air element dissolves.

These four appearances are perceived by relatively gross levels of the subtle mind. These four appearances are called the four signs of sleeping. During death we perceive the same four appearances more clearly.

After we perceive these signs, another four signs called the four empties arise. The first of these is the mind of white appearance. At this time everything is perceived as totally empty but white and bright. At this point the subtle mind of sleep develops and our mind becomes subtler and subtler.

The next of the four empties is the mind of red increase. The mind which perceives the red appearance is subtler than the previous levels of mind. This mind perceives everything as totally empty, but there is a red-coloured appearance. After this we perceive the mind of black near-attainment. Everything appears entirely empty but dark or black. During this stage we experience our deepest sleep.

After the black appearance the fourth empty arises — the mind of clear light. The dark appearance disappears and we perceive a clear light like the colour of dawn. This is called the clear light of sleep. There is no consciousness more subtle than the mind of clear light.

Just as we have more gross and more subtle levels of mind during sleep, likewise when we die we develop gross, subtle and very subtle levels of mind. At the last instant before death our mind perceives the clear light. If a person has the special good karma to be reborn as a human being, the continuum of that very subtle mind later enters into the union of the father's and mother's sperm and egg. From that time the mind becomes grosser and grosser.

If we examine the cell made from the union of sperm and egg, it is not obvious that there is a mind within. At the very beginning the body is like a liquid, like yogurt. But if that cell had no mind it would never develop; the very subtle consciousness which entered the mother's womb develops into gross consciousness like our present mind.

In cyclic existence our mental consciousness circles. It goes from one life to another. Because we took rebirth as a human being we experience the sufferings of a human being. If we were reborn as a horse or a fish we would experience the sufferings of those animals. Whatever kind of form we take, we will experience the sufferings of that form.

As long as we do not stop this cycle of death and rebirth there will be no end of suffering and dissatisfaction. Sooner or later we will experience the fears and miseries which are inherent in the nature of cyclic existence. The human mind can realize what is meant by samsara or cyclic existence and it can understand what the cause of taking rebirth in samsara is. The human mind can also understand what the method is which can cut this continuum of cyclic existence. Therefore it is very important to study the meaning of samsara, the method of attaining release from samsaric existence, and the meaning of nirvana or the state which is free from samsaric suffering.

If we seek the method of achieving nirvana or reaching other spiritual realizations, we are using our human capabilities fully. But if we concern ourself only with the considerations of this life, we are acting in a way that animals too can act. Some animals are very clever at destroying their enemies and protecting their friends and relatives. Some animals are very skilful in obtaining food for themselves or performing other actions such as building nests or homes. But animals have no opportunity to find the method for reaching nirvana.

The most intelligent animal cannot understand the meaning of nirvana, the difference between negative and positive actions, or how to meditate to reach Enlightenment. This is because it has taken rebirth as an animal. But the characteristic of human beings is that they can understand these things. Even if some of the terms used here, like subtle and very subtle consciousness, seem difficult to understand, if we think carefully about these teachings it is possible to understand them. Some Buddhist teachings are very profound and hard to understand, but if we exert great effort we can understand these subjects. If we cannot understand them completely at first, by thinking about the teachings they will become clearer and clearer. The teachings are like seeds which can slowly grow in the mind.

Thinking about these subjects opens our mind. We become more intelligent. Once our mind becomes flexible and open, we should start to meditate and practise on subjects such as emptiness. The true Buddhist teachings are very vast and profound and therefore require a great amount of time and effort to understand clearly. If we study the whole range of Buddhist teachings our attitudes will change and our understanding will deepen.

CHAPTER 8

THE FUNCTIONS OF MIND

The functions of mind are very extensive. Each human being has a different mind and each different mind has different functions. The minds of different animals also have different functions. Thus, the functions of the minds of all sentient beings are numberless; they could not be counted. Nevertheless, some of these mental functions will be explained in this chapter.

FEELING

Feeling is a mind which experiences either pleasure, unpleasure or indifference. For example, if we see a very beautiful form our mind becomes happy. When we meet attractive objects we develop pleasurable feelings. However, when we meet undesirable or unattractive objects we develop painful or unpleasurable feelings. A mind which experiences objects that are neither attractive nor unattractive develops indifferent feelings. Meeting with any of these three types of objects — attractive, unattractive or indifferent — causes the mental factor of feeling to arise.

All our actions are performed by our body, speech or mind. Aside from these 'three doors', no actions can be created. The results of our physical, verbal and mental actions are experienced by feeling. Therefore any mind which feels or experiences the fruit of any action is called feeling.

At the moment, for ordinary beings, feeling causes rebirth in cyclic existence. For instance, when we develop pleasurable feelings we develop attachment which creates karma for us to be reborn in samsara. If we experience painful feelings, we become angry and this angry mind creates karma for us to be reborn in samsara. Neutral or indifferent feelings cause us to develop ignorant self-grasping. This ignorant self-grasping also creates karma for us to be reborn in samsaric existence. Thus, for ordinary sentient beings such feelings create the karma to be reborn in cyclic existence.

Both Buddhist and some non-Buddhist schools of philosophy discovered that feeling causes rebirth in samsara. They then meditated on the cessation of feeling. Many masters tried to cease to develop any feelings. They tried not to perceive any objects and to remain mindless, without thoughts or feelings. But this meditation alone cannot liberate us from cyclic existence. Meditation on the cessation of feeling can help only for a short time. For example, if we have problems of attachment, meditating on the cessation of feeling can help us temporarily. The problem of anger or hatred can also be helped by doing meditation on the cessation of feeling.

Although meditation on the cessation of feeling is a practice common to both Buddhists and some non-Buddhists, Buddhists believe that meditation on the cessation of feeling alone is insufficient. This meditation cannot help us ultimately because the root of all our samsaric suffering is self-grasping. If we cannot eliminate this self-grasping we will still experience suffering. As explained above, meditation on the cessation of feeling can be helpful only for a short time; but in order to cut the root of suffering which is self-grasping, we must meditate on emptiness. It is stated in both the Sutra texts and in the Tantric Buddhist texts that without realizing emptiness we will not be able to stop self-grasping. Thus, if we cannot destroy our self-grasping we will remain in samsara.

It is important to know that the three kinds of feelings — pleasurable, unpleasurable and indifferent — cause suffering. The three different types of feelings exist because there are three types of objects: attractive, unattractive and indifferent. These three types of objects include all the objects which we encounter every day.

DISCERNMENT

Discernment is a mental factor which discriminates between different objects or between different aspects of the same object. The mind which discriminates, for instance, between what is a human being and what is an animal is discernment. Without the mental factor of discernment we could not discriminate between different objects.

Discernment can discriminate between objects because it holds the specific characteristics or signs of the objects. Each human being has different signs. For example, our mother has her own individual signs or characteristics. Through the mental factor of discernment which knows these signs we can recognize our mother.

During sleep we cannot discriminate between objects because at that time our discernment is not operating. Also, during the death process our discernment degenerates and cannot discriminate whether the people who crowd around our bed are our relatives or not.

There are two kinds of discernment: right discernment and wrong or mistaken discernment. Sometimes our discernment can be mistaken as when we recognize a friend, but it turns out to be someone else. We can develop many wrong discernments. Thinking that a negative action is a positive action is also wrong discernment. Thieves, for instance, think that stealing is a good action. Once they consider that stealing is advantageous, they try to steal many things. Had they realized that stealing is a negative action, the thieves would never have devoted their lives to it. But thieves have wrong discernment which leads them into negative actions.

There was once a poor family in India with many children. The father of the family was ill and unable to work. The mother had to look after her many children, and only the eldest child, a son, was able to support the family. For some time the eldest son worked and provided food for his family.

Then the son began to develop a negative attitude to his family. He felt that it was incorrect for him to give all his money to support his family. He thought that if he left his family and lived by himself he could use all his earnings for himself and he would have a good life. Eventually the son said to his father,

> 'I want to leave the family to live by myself.'

The father answered,

> 'If you go, we will not get any food. Please stay with us.'

Finally the son refused to live with his family any more and moved into his own house. After he had worked for a few years, he became quite wealthy. He decided that he needed a wife. He became attached to a woman who was married to another man and he tried to persuade her to come to live with him. The man showed all his gold to the woman and said,

> 'If you come to live with me, all my gold will be made into ornaments for you.'

The woman asked him where he kept his gold, and he showed her the place. The woman told her husband that the man had a great amount of gold and treasure. One day she said to her husband,

> 'Tonight I will go to his house and leave the door open. You can then come in, take all his gold, and run away with it.'

The woman went to the man's house and left the door open. At midnight her husband came, stole all the other man's treasures, and escaped into the forest. The man realized he had been robbed and leapt up without his clothes and followed the husband into the forest. In the forest he met a tiger which attacked and killed him.

This man's horrible death was the result of his two previous wrong discernments. The first wrong discernment was giving up his beneficial intentions toward his family and seeking only his own happiness. The second wrong discernment was becoming involved with someone else's wife. The man thought his wealth would bring him a good life, but because of his wrong discernment, instead of having a good life he was killed by a tiger and all his possessions were taken by others.

Thus, it is very important to have right discernment. If our original discernments are wrong, we will experience bad results. The functions of the mental factor discernment are very important and extensive.

INTENTION

The function of the mental factor intention is to move our mind toward an object. Intention enables us to perceive and realize objects. Without the mental factor intention our mind could not function or move toward an object. Just as the wind directs a candle's flame, so intention moves our mind toward an object.

When we are alone in our home our mind becomes distracted by different objects. Sometimes it is directed toward our job, or our family or financial situation. Our primary mind moves toward these different objects because of the mental factor intention. If we did not have the mental factor intention, our mind would not be able to think, perceive, realize, or remember anything.

Because the mental factor intention is the basis for all our wishes, it is responsible for creating all our karma. Our karma or actions can be divided into three types: mental, verbal and physical. We can see how each of these kinds of action depends upon our intention.

Mental action or mental karma is our mental factor intention. For example, if our mental factor intention focuses on an attractive form, then we develop the wish to obtain that object. If our intention focuses on an unattractive form, then the wish arises not to obtain that object. All of our desires develop because of the thoughts of our mental factor intention.

The reason why we sometimes develop harmful thoughts is because of our intention. First intention moves our mind on to the object, then the desire to harm others may arise. This kind of mental action is a negative mental action or mental karma. It is from this negative mental action that the negative actions of speech and body arise. If this negative motivation causes us to harm others physically or to kill them this is a negative physical action or karma. With the motivation of harming others, if we speak harshly or verbally abuse others, this is a negative action of speech. Karma can only be created by our three doors of body, speech and mind. Other than these there is no fourth door for creating karma.

Intention is also responsible for developing our wholesome mental actions. If we develop the wish to help or benefit others, this is a positive mental action or mental karma. If this beneficial motivation causes us to perform beneficial physical actions such as protecting others, giving them food, and so forth, this is positive physical karma. Likewise, if our beneficial motivation leads us to speak pleasing or kind words to others, this is a virtuous action of speech.

Thus, intention creates all our karma. For example, if we have created a killing action or karma, the root of this is our mental factor intention. It is the mental factor of intention which enables us to develop the wish to kill others. After we develop this wishing mind, then we may act physically to kill others. By investigating our actions in this way, we can see that they depend upon intention. If we know the entire process of intention, then we know the operation of cause and effect or the law of karma.

It is extremely important to know about karma and its results. Sometimes it is very helpful to think about karma; it can also be of great practical benefit. If we create bad actions or bad karma the result will be suffering. However, if we create wholesome or virtuous actions, the definite result of this wholesome karma will be happiness. Thinking about what the results of our actions will be will help us to avoid committing those actions which produce suffering and encourage us to perform those actions which produce happiness.

Wrong discernment may lead us into negative actions. Thinking that killing or stealing are good actions creates bad mental karma. Other negative conceptualizations such as denying rebirth, denying the existence of Buddhahood, or denying the existence of karma also produce negative mental karma. Whenever we develop negative thoughts this produces bad mental karma. We should judge our own mind and see whether we are creating good or bad mental actions.

There are three kinds of negative mental actions. The first is covetousness – wishing to obtain others' possessions. The second is wishing to harm others, and the third is holding wrong views. If we develop any of these three thoughts or mental actions we create negative mental karma.

The three non-virtuous physical actions are killing, stealing, and sexual misconduct. Committing any of these results is negative physical karma. There are four non-virtuous actions of speech: lying, slander, harsh words, and idle gossip. It is important to know these ten negative actions and to avoid committing them.

The effects of negative actions

If we commit negative actions, such as killing, we will receive four effects. The first is the ripening effect; the second is the effect similar to its experience. The third is the effect similar to its action, and the last one is the environmental effect. By committing just one negative action, we will produce all of these four effects.

The ripening effect of killing others is that in the next life one will obtain an inferior form such as that of an animal. The effect similar to the experience of killing is that even though one may obtain a human body in the next life, one will have a short life and many illnesses. One's body will become very weak and never maintain strength and health.

The effect similar to the action of killing is that in future whatever form one takes, whether as a human or other sentient being, one will have the tendency to kill others. Owing to the mental imprints and instincts from the previous life, one will naturally develop the thought of killing others.

The environmental effect of killing ripens on the place where one will take rebirth. One will be born in an unhealthy place where it will be difficult to find food and one will be very poor in material possessions. These four effects follow the creation of any non-virtuous action.

There are many human beings, but they do not all experience the same conditions. Some people have a very strong body, good health, a long life, plenty of food to eat and live in a place which is quite healthy. They have these good conditions because of their previous lives' good karma, their own positive actions.

Other human beings spend their lives miserably. They have little food to eat and live in an unhealthy place. The condition of their bodies is poor, and it is hard for them to find medicines. Their life span is shorter than that of other human beings and they have a strong tendency and desire to kill others. All these bad conditions are due to their previous lives' actions. If we consider karma and its effects carefully, it becomes clear that it is very important to create wholesome karma and to eliminate negative karma.

All the results we experience have two causes: substantial and contributing. The substantial cause is our past accumulation of good or bad actions. Without the substantial cause there could not be any effect. The contributing or circumstantial cause comprises the circumstances which permit our karma to come to fruition.

Some people work for the whole of their lives, but they remain very poor. Despite their strong desire to become rich and their hard work, they never obtain wealth. Other individuals do not work as hard, yet they accumulate wealth and have a very comfortable life. This difference in achievement depends upon karma. If all results depended only on external actions, then everyone who worked very hard would become rich. But this is not the case: even the results of hard work are uncertain. This shows that external factors or circumstantial causes do not determine our experiences because their principal cause is karma. Therefore we should reject negative actions or karma and practise positive actions.

In so far as killing is concerned, if we kill even the most insignificant animal this produces negative karma. Some philosophies or schools of thought consider that if we kill a being such as a fish, this is not a negative action and there will be no negative results. They think that a fish does not have a mind or does not experience suffering. But if we consider carefully, we can determine whether a fish has a mind.

It is not necessary to study Dharma in order to know if a fish has a mind; we can understand this from observation. We should consider how fishermen try to catch fish. The fishermen put food on a hook and then throw the hook into the water. When a fish sees the food it develops strong attachment to eating that food. It thinks that the food will be pleasant to eat. Thus, a fish which thinks that it sees something to eat must have a mind. A fish which develops the desire to eat and which approaches food must have a mind. If the fish did not have a mind, it would never approach the food on a hook because it would never develop any desire to eat that food. From this example we can understand that fish do have minds.

Likewise, if we examine what happens when a fish is caught, we can observe whether the fish has a mind. When the fish is pulled from the water on a hook, its body is bleeding and it thrashes about. At that time the fish has immense suffering. From observing the fish's actions and its suffering we can understand that the fish has a mind. Therefore, if we kill a fish we will receive the negative karma of killing.

If we kill any sentient being, that is, a being which has a mind, we will produce negative karma. It is not necessary just to accept the Buddhist teachings about this; rather we should see for ourself whether sentient beings such as insects and animals experience suffering. If we cause any sentient being to suffer we will create negative karma. Thus, whether a sentient being is large or small, we should avoid injuring or killing it.

CONTACT

The contact referred to here is not physical contact, but mental contact. The mental factor contact develops because of the meeting of the object, the sense faculty and the consciousness. When the object, the sense faculty and the consciousness meet, it is the mental factor contact which knows the object for what it is. Without the mind of contact we could never know if an object was attractive or not.

It is because of contact that feeling develops. When the mental factor contact perceives an object as being beautiful we develop pleasurable feelings. In the same way, if the mental factor contact knows an object as indifferent or unattractive, then we will experience indifferent or unpleasurable feelings. Thus, contact is defined as a mind which knows an object as attractive, unattractive or indifferent because of the meeting of the sense faculty, the consciousness and the object.

ATTENTION

The mental factor attention is a mind which focuses on one particular object from among various objects. This focusing of the mind is the function of attention. For example, if we concentrate our mind on one person from among a group of people, this is the functioning of our mental factor attention. Without attention there could be no strong concentration.

SLEEP

If we consider sleep, strictly speaking, sleep is a mind. There are many ways to dissolve our five sense consciousnesses and five sense faculties inwards. Sometimes owing to external conditions the five sense faculties are gathered inwardly. Illnesses such as epilepsy or fainting can cause our five sense faculties to gather inwardly for a short time. Also, at the time of death the five sense faculties are gathered or dissolved inwardly. During these times of illness or death a person has a mind, but that mind is never called sleep. Only a mind which develops from the natural gathering of the five sense faculties inwards is called sleep.

The mind of sleep is sometimes wholesome and sometimes unwholesome; but usually it is indifferent. It changes frequently between these states. The mental factor sleep is a type of mind which is a little subtler than our normal waking mind. When we are awake, the different minds which arise can use memory because they are gross minds. Because the mind of sleep is a relatively subtle mind, it cannot use recollection. However, through the force of meditation it is possible for some beings to use their memory during sleep. But in general ordinary beings cannot do this.

REGRET

Regret can be either a wholesome, unwholesome or neutral mind. Regret is a mind which feels sorrow or remorse about past actions. The nature of the regret depends on the nature of the action we feel sorry for having committed. For instance, if we feel regret for past negative actions such as killing, stealing, sexual misconduct and so forth, this is positive regret. Regretting non-virtuous actions is a wholesome mind.

Negative regret, in contrast, is an unwholesome mind which feels sorry for past virtuous actions. For example, feeling regret that we have received Dharma teachings or performed wholesome meditations is negative regret. Regretting any kind of positive action such as practising patience, helping others, and so forth is negative regret.

In addition to positive and negative regret, there is also indifferent regret. This is a mind which regrets an indifferent or neutral action. If we feel regret, for example, just for eating, this is indifferent regret.

INVESTIGATION

The mental factor investigation is a mind which examines objects superficially, without making a precise examination. The object of investigation can be any object — wholesome, unwholesome or indifferent.

There are two kinds of meditation: analytical meditation and placement meditation. Analytical meditation can be further divided into two types: rough analytical meditation and precise analytical meditation. The nature of rough analytical meditation, investigating the object of meditation in a rough or general way, is the mind of investigation.

ANALYSIS

The mental factor analysis is a mind which investigates its object carefully and precisely. As in the case of the mental factor investigation, the object can be either wholesome, unwholesome or indifferent.

The nature of precise analytical meditation is the mind of analysis. Precise examination applies not only to meditation. If we read a book precisely, this is analysis. If we reason precisely, this is also the mental factor analysis. After receiving Dharma teachings, if we investigate them roughly, this is the mind of investigation; but if we investigate them carefully and in depth, this is the mind of analysis.

The mental factors of investigation and analysis apply to worldly as well as spiritual actions. For instance, if we wish to harm others and we consider in a rough way how to accomplish this, this is an unwholesome mind of investigation. If we consider precisely a method to harm others, this is an unwholesome mind of analysis. In the same way, wholesome or indifferent minds arise when these two changeable mental factors focus on wholesome or indifferent objects.

All the mental factors explained here should be distinguished by the difference in their functions. Their functions are different, but they are all the same in that they are all mind. All of these different mental factors are aspects of our mind.

At first it may be difficult to understand these different mental factors or minds. But in the same way that a mechanic can understand all of the functions of a complicated machine or engine by studying them, by studying continuously we can understand all of the functions of our different minds more clearly. The reason why we can understand these minds such as feelings, discernment, sleep and regret is because we have all of these minds within us. If we investigate, study, and train ourself, we can understand our mind. Just as scientists examine external or physical phenomena, we should examine our inner mind. There is a time-honoured Tibetan saying that if we wish to observe a spectacle we should watch our own mind. It is exceedingly important to investigate our mind and to make it very strong and positive.

HAPPINESS DEPENDS ON THE MIND

Happiness depends on our mind. It is very important to understand this. We might think that to assert that happiness is developed internally is incorrect, that it involves contradictions. But, by investigating carefully, we can see that it is true.

In general, people believe that happiness depends on wealth and possessions, on having friends or a good social position. For ordinary beings this kind of view is correct. That is, ordinary beings do depend on external things like wealth and social status for their happiness. Without these things most people would not be happy because they would not be able to understand the situation in terms of Dharma.

Because ordinary beings don't know how to develop happiness mentally, it may seem that for such beings happiness depends only on external conditions. This is a relative kind of happiness, not ultimate happiness. Superficially it may appear that the existence of this relative happiness, a happiness which depends on wealth, possessions, a good job, etc., contradicts the assertion that happiness arises from inside and depends only upon the mind. But actually these two views of happiness are complementary rather than contradictory. Even happiness which seems to depend on external causes in reality also depends on one's mind.

For example, someone who receives a large amount of money will experience happiness. But if we investigate precisely, what is it that experiences happiness? It is the mental factor feeling which causes the person to experience happiness. Without the mind of feeling no amount of wealth could bring about the experience of happiness. Even if we carefully water a field, if there are no seeds in the ground there can never be any crops in that field. In a similar manner, even though someone may receive a large sum of money, if there is no strong development of feeling there will be no happiness. This situation is like the field where there are no seeds, but only water.

There are some people who hold important positions and possess many material goods, but despite their wealth and power they are not happy. Instead they have terrible suffering which may even lead them to suicide. Although such people are very rich externally, they have no strong development of positive feeling. They lack a strong development of positive feeling because mentally they are very poor.

It sometimes happens that someone dies and leaves a great deal of money to a dog or a cat. The animal will never experience happiness from this wealth because it develops no strong feeling about it. Thus, we can see that happiness depends not just on external causes such as wealth, but also on our feeling and other similar minds. If we consider this carefully, we can understand that our happiness depends on our mind.

Many realized Tibetan meditators, such as Milarepa, spent many years in barren caves where they had few possessions and little food. Despite these harsh external conditions they experienced immense happiness. This indicates that happiness is something which exists internally and depends on one's inner feeling. We should examine the way that these meditators developed strong internal happiness and, if possible, we should try to experience this internal happiness ourself.

There was once an old, wrinkled Tibetan lama who was very poor in material possessions. He said,

> 'Others see me as withered, old and poor; but internally I have inexpressible happiness.'

To some people it might appear that the old lama was being proud or boasting of his attainments; but what he meant was that his happiness was not created by any external cause. His happiness was derived from his meditations, his attitude, and his Dharma practice.

If we think about mental factors and their functions this will help to develop our mind. Contemplating how happinesss depends on our mind will assist us in striving to develop lasting internal happiness. Thinking about these subjects increases our wisdom.

CHAPTER 9

EQUANIMITY

At present our mind is not generally unbiased or very stable toward others. This is because when we encounter unattractive objects such as someone we dislike or an enemy, anger and aversion tend to arise. Also, when we meet an attractive object such as a relative or friend we tend to develop attachment, and when we encounter an indifferent or neutral object such as a stranger we develop neutral feelings. This indicates that our mind is not very balanced.

Some people experience immense anger or develop overbearing attachment and often suffer from other painful mental states because of their biased minds. We should try to cultivate a balanced, unbiased mind toward others in order to avoid these painful mental states. In the Mahayana tradition, if we wish to attain the realization of equanimity, this unbiased mind is indispensable.

The great master Je Tsong Khapa said that equanimity is like the ground or field, great compassion is like the seed, love is like water, the altruistic mind of bodhicitta and other Mahayana paths are like the plants, and Buddhahood is like the fruit. The fruit of Enlightenment is dependent on the altruistic mind of bodhicitta and the mind of bodhicitta depends on the seed-like great compassionate mind. The compassionate mind depends upon water-like love, and love depends on the field-like equanimity. Equanimity, therefore, is the foundation of all Mahayana spiritual realizations, including the precious bodhicitta.

In order to develop any spiritual insight it is important to develop equanimity. We often develop love for our relatives and friends, but hardly ever for our enemies or those we dislike. We find it difficult to develop love for persons other than our relatives and friends. But most of the love which we direct to our friends and relatives is mixed with attachment. This mixture of attachment and love is not the result of Dharma realizations. In the Mahayana tradition, love should be cultivated for all beings without discrimination.

The mind which feels a closeness to all beings in this way is the supreme mind of love. A person who has this love for all beings without discrimination is not a very ordinary person. It is certain that such a person holds inner realizations within his or her consciousness. When someone who possesses this kind of love meets or sees others, a natural and spontaneous feeling of happiness arises. Such a person never develops an angry or jealous mind, and as a result of this everyone will become that person's friend, holding him or her in great respect. A person who practises love purely will also as a result have a very peaceful mind.

Once love has been developed, it is then not very hard to develop the realizations of compassion and bodhicitta or other spiritual realizations. In order to generate love for all sentient beings, our mind must first be equalized. Without first equalizing the mind it is very difficult to develop love for all sentient beings.

MEDITATION ON EQUANIMITY

If we develop anger toward one person and attachment toward another, this shows that we still hold discriminations; and therefore it will be very hard for us to attain the realization of love directed equally to all beings. It is essential, at first, to equalize our mind. Without depending on a method or remedy it is very difficult to develop an unbiased mind. We should try to achieve equanimity through a practical method of meditation.

Overcoming anger

The first stage is to try to overcome our anger and jealousy for our enemies. We should try to visualize our enemies and people whom we dislike, for example someone who may have tried to harm us in the past, the mere thought of whom immediately causes anger to arise within our mind. Visualizing such a person as vividly as possible in front of us, we should consider how this person we now dislike has been our mother and close friend in many previous lives. We feel closeness and affection for our present mother because we were born from her womb and were cared for by her, but she is not the only mother we have had. The continuum of our consciousness stretches back over infinite time and the number of births we have experienced during this time is countless. Just as we have been born countless times, we have also had countless mothers.

There is not a single being that we meet who, over this incalculable span of time without beginning, has not at one time or another been our mother. Our present mother showed us inexhaustible kindness by selflessly carrying us in her womb for nine months and being ever concerned for our welfare. Even though our birth caused her intense pain, still she thought only of our happiness and well-being.

As a helpless infant we received great care for our mother: she fed us with her milk and constantly cleaned the excrement from our dirty body. As we grew older into adult life, she protected us from many dangers; she rejoiced in our happiness and shared our sorrows. Without her constant care and attention it would be doubtful if we would still be alive – such is our mother's kindness and love.

From beginningless time countless mothers have shown us this same limitless care and love. We should now consider how the enemy we are visualizing in front of us has been our mother, nurturing and caring for us with selfless love many times in the past.

If we have no belief in past lives, then this practice is very hard to actualize. If we have an interest in studying Buddhism it is beneficial to accept the belief in former lives. But if doubts do occur about regarding other beings as having been our mother, it may be helpful to reread the chapter 'Reincarnation'.

If there was a former life, there must have been a life before that one and a life before that; this process is endless. Because our former lives stretch back endlessly, we cannot say with certainty that the enemy we are now visualizing has never in a previous life been our friend or mother. The great pandit Nagarjuna said that our rebirth is unfixed: our present mother may become our wife in a future rebirth; we may become the wife of our present mother. Our present mother may have been our son in a past life. The form of our future rebirths is totally indefinite and unfixed.

The Buddha stated that our reincarnations are like actors on a stage who appear in different ways and different costumes while they act out their different roles. The Buddha said that the person who may now be an enemy has been parent, son, daughter and friend in the past. Even if we doubt that our present enemy has been our mother in a past life, it is certain that this person has been our friend at one time.

Even in this present life our relationships are not fixed. Often in our school days we may have a particular enemy who causes us to feel hatred within our mind. But in our later life the same person may become our closest friend or our husband or wife. Likewise, a person who was our dearest friend may, through the circumstances of life, change into our greatest enemy. Our own experiences in this present life show how easily enemies can become friends and friends can become enemies. If our friends and enemies change so frequently in this lifetime, how many times in our countless past lives have our friends and enemies changed places? Since our enemies and friends constantly change, we should contemplate how many times our present enemy must have been our friend.

We should realize that the enemy we have visualized is not permanent, but has in numerous past lives helped us in many ways, showing us all the loving-kindness of a close friend. Therefore we have no reason for allowing anger to arise toward this person. Thinking in this way, we should make a strong determination from our heart that from now on we will never let anger or jealousy develop in our mind toward others; instead we will always bear in mind the loving-kindness they have shown us in countless past lives.

Having made this determination, we should then focus our mind single-pointedly on this in meditation. When we have finished our meditation we should try to be mindful and to maintain the same determination not to become angry or jealous which we developed during meditation. Finally, we should resolve that when in daily life we come into contact with our enemies or people we dislike, for instance, someone who speaks harshly of our relatives or friends or someone who holds different political views, we will not develop anger.

All such people or enemies become objects for our meditation. We should consider how these people have benefited and cared for us in the past. For a short period someone may treat us badly, but this is insignificant compared to the help and kindness this person has shown by being our mother or friend in many past lives.

Because the roles of enemy and friend interchange so frequently, even within one lifetime, there is no real reason to become angry with an enemy, for it is certain that he or she has treated us with great kindness in the past. Furthermore, there is no doubt that circumstances will again change, causing our enemy to become our friend again in the future. Having understood this, we should make a strong determination never to become angry at the negative attitudes of others' minds. If we engage in this form of meditation every day with good motivation, we will never experience the problems of an angry or jealous mind.

It is often helpful to reflect on the disadvantages of negative states of mind, such as anger and jealousy, in order to overcome them. The root cause of war in the world today is the anger and jealousy we hold in our minds. Whether there are disputes between individuals, political factions or nations, the root cause remains the same. Clearly, if everyone practised meditation on equanimity – not allowing anger or jealousy to develop – there would be peace throughout the world.

From a general point of view, it would be very beneficial if societies overcame anger, creating a more stable and peaceful environment in which to live. From an individual point of view, it is extremely important to overcome anger and other negative forces such as grudge-holding and jealousy. If we can avert the development of anger through the force of our meditation, this is the fruit of our meditation on equanimity. If we should come into contact with an enemy or person we previously disliked and now find that aversion or anger does not arise, our meditation is proving successful.

Overcoming attachment

Many problems are also experienced because of attachment; therefore when attachment arises we should try to apply this equanimity meditation in reverse. That is, instead of considering how an enemy becomes a friend, we should consider how a friend also becomes an enemy.

If we experience problems because of overbearing attachment to another person, we should visualize that object of attachment in front of us. We should now consider how this very person has been our enemy many times in countless previous lives. We should consider, for example, how he or she has spoken many harsh words against us, how this person has stolen from and physically harmed or even killed us and mutilated our body countless times in the past. Thinking that this person has been the cause of much suffering for us in the past, what reason is there to be so attached to him or her? We should then end the meditation with a strong determination that there is no longer any reason to be so attracted and attached to this person. By reducing attachment through this meditation, we can solve the problems that attachment produces.

Many years ago there was a beautiful girl named Chandra who lived within the closely knit community of a small village. Because of her beauty, the majority of the youths of the village were very attracted to Chandra. Through their rivalry much fighting and many disputes and problems arose.

These problems became so severe for Chandra that she finally went to seek the counsel of a wise and learned guru who, upon hearing about her problems, gave her teachings on Dharma. After receiving these teachings, Chandra invited all of the youths in her village to gather around her. Chandra explained to them how, in previous lives, she had been their enemy and had harmed and killed them many times. She also went on to explain how she had stolen their treasures, causing them great suffering in numerous past lives.

Then Chandra said,

> 'I have been your enemy many times. Is there any reason why, simply because in this life my form has changed, you have become so attached to me?'

Upon hearing this, the young men who were gathered around her realized that what Chandra had explained was true; and because of this their attachment was greatly reduced and did not trouble Chandra as it had in the past. This shows that if the speaker is skilful and the listeners receptive, just by giving a short discourse on Dharma the speaker can reduce the delusions which are in the listeners' minds.

The uncertainty of cyclic existence

There are many true stories illustrating how one's enemies are unfixed and uncertain or changing. The Buddha had a close disciple called Shariputra who had highly developed supernatural powers such as clairvoyance and intuition. While Shariputra was meditating on a high mountain, he perceived clairvoyantly the activities of a family in the valley below. He also gained insight into their past lives.

At first the family consisted of the father and mother (now both deceased) and their son. Shariputra observed that in the past the father of the family had a very strong desire and attraction for fishing in a pond behind his house. Because of his strong attachment to fishing and to the pond behind his house, when the father died he was reborn in that same pond as a fish.

When the father's wife, the mother of the son, died she developed immense attachment to her home. After her death she was reborn as a dog which was a pet of the same family.

When the father and his wife were still alive taking care of their son, they had one particular enemy who had a strong attachment to the wife and who caused many problems for the family. This enemy also died and was later reborn as the son of their son.

The father of the new son, like his father before him, had a strong attraction to fishing and on this day decided to go fishing in the same pond that his father had been so fond of. His attempts to catch a fish were successful, but unknowingly he caught the fish which was the reincarnation of his father. He then took the fish which was previously his father back to his home, where his wife fried and prepared it for eating.

Shariputra then observed with considerable amusement the drama of this family scene. The man took on his lap his baby son who, in a past life, was his family's enemy; he also began to eat the fish which in reality was his father. The dog — which had been his mother — then became excited and began to wag its tail at the prospect of receiving scraps of the fish. The man kicked the dog as it tried to jump on him to obtain food.

Seeing these workings of karma, Shariputra laughed even more and began to compose a short stanza about what he had seen:

> The man is eating his own father's flesh
> And kicking his mother;
> He is keeping his enemy on his lap —
> I laugh at the conditions of samsara.

The stanza was a teaching about the uncertainty of cyclic existence.

Our friends and enemies are unfixed and our present relationships with them will inevitably change. Therefore we have no real reason to regard a friend with attachment and an enemy with aversion. By abandoning these two negative extremes we are capable of equalizing our biased mind, making it unbiased.

We should try to abandon all forms of anger for our enemies and overcome strong attachment for our friends. If possible, we should hold the same equal mind for both objects. If we can achieve this equal mind for both friends and enemies, then of course it is easy to develop this mind for all beings — friends, enemies and strangers. If we can accomplish this we will have developed the realization of equanimity. Once we have developed the realization of equanimity, it is not very difficult to develop love, great compassion, and the mind of bodhicitta.

If we develop a strong feeling of equanimity by reflecting on these points, we should then meditate single-pointedly on equanimity without losing this feeling which we have generated. When we eventually arise from our meditation, we should try to remember these same points and this feeling of equanimity toward all beings. If we engage in this meditation constantly our mind will become very stable and it will be difficult for attachment or aversion to develop toward others.

At the moment it is very difficult for us to have a completely stable and unmoving mind. We are often joyfully happy and then within a short period of time we become extremely morose and sad. This indicates that our mind is not generally balanced, but changes constantly and indiscriminately from one mental state to another. Instead of this see-saw mind, we should try to cultivate a neutral mind which is neither over-happy nor over-sad. This means that we should retain an equalizing state of mind. Whether the circumstances we meet are extremely good or extremely bad, our mind remains the same. Our mind should be unchanging, like a mountain which can never be moved by the wind.

For those who develop this unmoving, mountain-like mind, there are naturally fewer problems and these people are not easily swayed by the ever-changing circumstances of life. Meditations such as this one on equanimity can be very useful in daily life and help us greatly in solving the unending problems we face. Most of our mental problems are the result of our over-busy mind.

Meditation can be likened to a medicine which can cure the problems within our mind. When we are unhappy, angry or jealous, for example, meditation can help to calm our mind. Therefore, it is very beneficial to be familiar with the techniques of meditation which can help us in daily life. By being born as a human being we have a great advantage: the ability to meditate. Animals such as dogs cannot meditate, no matter how intelligent they appear to be. Dogs may be able to learn to respond in a certain way through training, but they are not able to understand Dharma.

By virtue of meditation and Dharma practice, a human being can become Enlightened whereas animals and beings of the lower realms do not have this ability. To receive a human rebirth is indeed rare; but to receive a human rebirth and come into contact with the Mahayana teachings, and to be able to meditate upon them is rarer still. Since we have now met the Mahayana teachings we should not let this opportunity be lost.

MEDITATION POSTURE: THE POSTURE HAVING THE SEVEN FEATURES OF BUDDHA VAIROCHANA'S WAY OF SITTING

When we engage in meditation it is advantageous to adopt the traditional or formal posture. This posture has been used by many great yogis of both ancient and modern times and has great significance.

1 The legs

If possible, the legs should be crossed in the full vajra position. The left foot is first placed sole upwards on the right thigh, and then the right foot is placed sole upwards on the left thigh so that the right leg is crossed over the left. However, if we find the full cross-legged vajra position difficult, we should adopt the half-vajra position, placing the right foot sole upwards on the left thigh with the left leg crossed beneath it. We should sit on a cushion which will slightly raise the back part of our body. If we find the half-vajra position difficult, then we can simply sit on a chair or in any other way which we find more comfortable.

2 The hands

The right hand should be placed on top of the left hand with both palms facing upwards. The two thumbs should be touching, and the hands should be placed close to the body with the thumbs at the level of the navel. This is the posture of meditative equipoise.

3 The back

The back should be absolutely straight. If the whole trunk is kept as straight as possible it keeps the spine straight. This helps the mind to remain clear and alert.

4 The teeth and lips

The teeth and lips should be closed in their normal position, neither open nor too tightly closed. The tongue should be set against the back of the upper teeth which will prevent the mouth from becoming too dry.

5 The head

The head should be inclined slightly downwards; this helps to overcome mental excitement.

6 The eyes

The eyes should be half-open, neither wide open nor completely closed. If we close our eyes we may become sleepy or experience mental sinking. We should not look straight ahead but down at the tip of our nose without actually concentrating on it.

7 The shoulders

The shoulders should be straight, level and balanced.

It is very important before we start our meditation to develop the correct motivation. If we were to meditate out of a negative motivation such as wishing to gain praise or rewards for ourself, this would not be at all helpful to our spiritual development. Before we engage in meditation we need a wholesome motivation such as wishing to help and protect others in order to produce any benefit.

After we have completed our meditation, it is important to dedicate the meritorious power which we have generated through our meditation to a wholesome goal. If we dedicate our merit to a wholesome purpose such as realizing equanimity, freeing all sentient beings from their sufferings, or attaining Enlightenment in order to lead all sentient beings to that supreme state, that merit will never be lost until the goal is achieved.

BASIC BREATHING MEDITATION

The object of our meditation is, of course, a matter for personal choice and subject to our own needs or scope. If we are unable to engage in higher forms of meditation, we should at least be able to perform basic breathing techniques.

At first we should concentrate on our normal inhalations and exhalations of breath through our nostrils, and in this way we will find that a new sensation inside the nose is generated. Without losing this sensation we should focus our mind single-pointedly on the breath inside our nostrils.

Breathing meditations such as this are initially helpful in overcoming our distractions and unhappy states of mind.

CHAPTER 10

LOVE

Love has the power of bestowing temporal happiness upon us in this lifetime. If something is capable of bringing about our happiness, it is only sensible to adopt such a practice. Therefore we should practise love for others. Even if our love is mixed with attachment it can still be beneficial. Whether we are religious or not, practising love is very important.

To give an indication of the powerful effect that love can have on our happiness, let us consider a common example. Sometimes we may observe a married couple who are materially very poor, yet somehow their lives seem to be very happy. They have a deep understanding between them. When we consider the basis of their fulfilling relationship, we find that their happiness is based on the foundation of love. Even if a married couple have all the material comforts they desire, without the foundation of love for each other they will have dissatisfaction, poor communication and much mental suffering.

If there is no love between people, it is definite that problems will occur. From our own experience we can all see that this applies not only to husbands and wives, but also to families, friends, and even nations. If, for example, a group of people who live together as a community practise love toward each other, then they will enjoy happiness as a result. However, if they have no practice of love at all, many complications will develop. Angry or jealous states of mind which can sometimes lead to actual hatred of one another will arise.

If people never had angry minds there would be no foundation for disputes and conflicts. The Buddha said that if we have no practice of love for each other there can be no positive or Dharma effect. Practising love is therefore the pledge of all Buddhists. Each religion has different pledges or commitments, and even within the two Buddhist paths of Sutra and Tantra there are many pledges of varying degrees. However, the Mahayana Buddhist has three main commitments: the first of these is to practise love; the second is to work for the benefit and welfare of others; and the third is to take refuge in the Buddha. Whoever abides by these three pledges purely is a very holy person and a true Buddhist.

Buddhism itself refers to the attitude and actions of a person, not to the robes or particular style of dress that he or she may be wearing. The difference between a Buddhist and a non-Buddhist is not their robes or style of dress; it is the attitude or motivation within the person's mind. Buddhists of different schools and countries often wear different robes, some red, some white or yellow, depending upon the customs and conditions of the country in which they live. From the mere external appearance of robes, one cannot say whether a person is a Buddhist or not. Neither can one say whether or not someone is a Buddhist because of his or her diet or way of eating. Tibetan Buddhists eat Tibetan food, Indian Buddhists eat Indian food, and Western Buddhists eat food which is particular to a Western life style or climate.

Buddhism is defined in terms of the way a person thinks and acts. However, whether or not someone is a Buddhist, it is very important for everyone to practise love toward others. Love nourishes our inner development and is the source of all happiness.

Seeing the benefits and potential power of love, we should try to develop and practise it. Even if we do not have the full capability of practising love now, we should try to gain this and gradually increase our level or scope of practice. If someone should have no love at all, he or she should try to cultivate it by contemplating the benefits that love can bring and the disadvantages of not developing this wholesome state of mind.

There are two types of love. One is very strong but is limited in the length of time that it lasts, whereas the other is also strong, but lasts over a much longer duration of time. This second type of love holds much greater benefits than the first type. It is much more balanced and therefore more lasting. An example of this second type of love is the love that a mother displays for her child. This closeness and warmth of the mother's love usually lasts throughout her entire lifetime. The first type of love, in contrast, may last only for a short period — a matter of years, months, or even weeks. After this type of love fades, disharmony will develop and difficulties in communication will arise.

It is therefore very important to have lasting love that is both stable and strong. If our love is strong but unstable, it will not last over a long period. In the same way, a heavy downpour of rain can create many temporary new rivers and streams. These new rivers and streams may have a very strong effect over a short time, but this effect is not lasting and will subside when the downpour has stopped. Likewise, if we have no enduring love our relationships with others will be unstable, like a married couple whose initial strong love soon subsides. Our love should be constant like a river that has always been present and will always remain.

THE UNCOMMON PRACTICE OF LOVE

The uncommon practice of love is developed within the Mahayana tradition. This practice is to develop love for all beings and to cherish others more than oneself, without self-interest or attachment.

For someone who is unfamiliar with Dharma and the Mahayana tradition it may be difficult to understand this second aspect of love. However, for someone who is becoming familiar with the Mahayana tradition or who has positive tendencies carried over from a past life, accepting these teachings and developing love for all beings is not very difficult. If we have the desire to reach the fully awakened state of Buddhahood in this very lifetime, we must enter into the Mahayana tradition. Without spiritually depending on the Mahayana or Great Vehicle it is impossible to attain full Enlightenment.

Followers of the Hinayana tradition or Lesser Vehicle may attain liberation, freedom from the sufferings of samsara, through the virtue of their pure practices, but it is not possible to attain full Enlightenment without entering into the Mahayana tradition and engaging in its practices. It can be extremely beneficial to enter the Mahayana tradition, and therefore we should direct our energy and effort toward this goal. Because we now have a precious human form and have also encountered the Mahayana tradition, we now have the opportunity to embark upon the actual Mahayana path.

If we do not cultivate precious Mahayana minds such as great love — love for all sentient beings — and practise these teachings now, a very rare opportunity indeed will have been lost. If we were to find a precious gem and then throw it away without knowing its true value, a chance to benefit ourself would be lost. Equally, if we come into contact with the precious Mahayana teachings and do not use the opportunity to our advantage, we may later be filled with regret at not having done so, by which time it may also be too late.

If we meet the right conditions at the right time, when our sense faculties are sharp and strong, and then pass up this opportunity to practise Dharma, we may find that if in later life we again wish to meet the teachings and practise Dharma, the opportunity may no longer be available. We may be too old and frail; we may be too late and experience great regret for not having taken the opportunity when we could. Therefore we should put great effort into the practice of Dharma now; otherwise the opportunity to do so may soon disappear.

Receiving a chance to enter the Mahayana tradition and practise the Mahayana path is a tremendous privilege. A great Kadampa Geshe was once asked whether he would rather choose to fly in the sky and possess clairvoyance or practise the Mahayana path. The Geshe replied that in many of his previous lives he had the ability to fly in the sky and also in many previous existences he developed clairvoyance, seeing many different things that were beyond the normal eye. The realized Geshe then went on to explain that if he had practised the Mahayana teachings in his previous lives his situation would have completely changed and he would no longer be experiencing the sufferings of cyclic existence.

The Geshe further explained that he was truly fortunate to have met the Mahayana teachings and a Mahayana teacher in his present life. He preferred the Mahayana teachings to the pursuit of levitation and so forth because the Mahayana teachings offered him the opportunity to attain full Enlightenment in his present life. Once he had attained full Enlightenment, he would naturally have numberless abilities such as flying in the sky which would require no special effort to perform. For these reasons the Geshe concluded that the Mahayana teachings were superior.

One of the main Mahayana practices is to develop concentration on love by focusing our attention on other beings. To practise and gain such concentration on love by using other beings as our object of meditation is supreme among all the Mahayana practices. The reason why this practice is supreme can be illustrated by Shakyamuni Buddha's own experience.

When Shakyamuni Buddha was about to achieve final Enlightenment, many Maras or demons tried to kill him by using various weapons. It is said that thousands of demons tried to harm him and prevent his Enlightenment. As the Maras tried to disturb him, the Buddha developed immutable concentration on love, and despite the Maras' activities they were unable to disturb the Buddha's meditation.

The Maras' weapons, arrows and so forth, which they employed against the Buddha were transformed into flowers through the force of the Buddha's concentration on love. When the Maras saw that the Buddha could not be harmed by these means, they tried to disturb his concentration by manifesting themselves as beautiful women. But even though they manifested in very attractive forms, the Maras failed to interrupt the Buddha's meditation.

Through the force of the Buddha's concentration on love he attained full Enlightenment on the fifteenth day of the fourth month, according to the Tibetan calendar. If we can practise love purely, even if at first our concentration is not as good as that of Buddha Shakyamuni, we will definitely experience beneficial results and eventually we will attain the Buddha's immutable love.

THE EIGHT BENEFITS OF PRACTISING LOVE

There are eight benefits which result from the practice of love. The first of these eight benefits is that the practitioner will gain strong meritorious power. Giving love to all beings has greater benefit than giving them food. This is because practising love purely causes us to reach Enlightenment quickly. Giving beings food may be of temporary benefit in alleviating their hunger, but this lasts only a few hours until they again require food. By reaching Enlightenment quickly through increasing our meritorious power, we obtain the power skilfully to lead all sentient beings from suffering into the same Enlightened state. Love, therefore, has the ultimate benefit of bestowing meritorious power.

The second benefit is that if love is practised sincerely, humans and gods will return love and respect to the practitioner. The reason why they return love and respect to the practitioner is that actions produce a result similar to their cause. If we plant seeds of love, then according to the law of karma we will also receive the fruit of love.

The third benefit of practising love is that humans and gods will provide protection from obstacles to our health, life, and so forth. Fourth, by practising love our mind will always remain calm and peaceful. The fifth benefit of practising love is that we will experience physical comfort and flexibility.

The sixth benefit is that if other beings try to harm the practitioner, for example, by administering poison or using weapons, this will have no effect. If our concentration is very developed it is impossible to receive harm from others. The seventh benefit which results from practising love is that we will be reborn as a Deva in the higher, more fortunate god realms.

Finally, the eighth benefit of practising love is that in the future whoever looks upon or has contact with the practitioner of love will find him or her to be pleasant and attractive. In addition, through practising love all of our wishes will be fulfilled.

If we continue to practise love, cherishing others more than ourself, we will develop great compassion for all beings. In order to develop this mind of great compassion, we should resolve to practise love in accordance with the Mahayana tradition. Without depending on a method such as one taught within the Mahayana tradition, we cannot develop love for all sentient beings automatically, without any cause. Therefore we must first know and strive to practise a method for developing love before we can receive the benefits of practising love.

There are three methods to gain the realization of love. The first method is to see the benefits which come about through cherishing other beings. The second method is to see the faults and disadvantages of a self-cherishing mind, and the third method is to remember the kindness of other beings.

THE BENEFITS OF CHERISHING OTHERS

If we seriously contemplate these three methods of reasoning, it is certain that we will eventually attain the realization of love. We should begin with the first of these methods: seeing the benefits that come about through cherishing others. It is generally impossible for us to realize fully the benefits of cherishing others without studying Dharma teachings, such as the eight benefits explained earlier. We should consider, for example, the effects produced by the Buddha when he engaged in the practice of cherishing others.

Long before Buddha Shakyamuni became Enlightened he was in every way an ordinary sentient being. Through coming into contact with the Mahayana teachings and, in particular, practising love, he finally reached the state of full Enlightenment. It is very important at first to develop our own practice of love by contemplating how the Buddha cherished others. If we have a strong desire to know in detail how the Buddha practised cherishing others, we should read some of the many biographies that are available about his life. One example will be given below.

In one of the Buddha's previous lives he was reborn as a king known as Pemachen. At the time of King Pemachen's reign his country was facing a severe epidemic. The epidemic was so serious that all who became diseased quickly died, and the doctors could find no cure. As a result of this epidemic which was sweeping King Pemachen's country, many thousands of people died within the space of one month. King Pemachen could see that if a cure was not soon found, most of his subjects would certainly die.

The king called a council of many doctors and instructed them to make new efforts to find a cure for the disease. Despite the doctors' efforts, no cure could be found. However, one doctor explained that there was once a cure for the disease that could be made by extracting certain substances from the body of a very rare fish called a rohita. The doctor explained that this fish could only be found in the doctor's homeland on a distant shore and that he had already spent many years trying to find this medicinal fish. He had not succeeded and therefore now believed the rohita to be extinct. After hearing this, the king returned to his palace and thought deeply.

The king reasoned that if the epidemic were to continue, he and his subjects would soon be likely to die; and if he could no longer serve his people, then there was no great benefit in keeping his present body. He resolved that he must die and try to benefit his people by taking rebirth as the rare medicinal fish to save them from disease. Having developed this strong motivation to benefit others, he called for the doctor who had previously searched for the rohita and instructed him to return to the distant sea and renew his search.

The doctor again explained that his years of searching had produced no sign of the medicinal fish and that even if he were to find one, this would not be sufficient to cure everyone of the disease. King Pemachen nevertheless insisted that the doctor depart immediately and renew his search. The king advised the doctor that if he found one fish there would be more.

The very same night, after the doctor departed on his journey, King Pemachen died and was subsequently reborn as he had wished, as a rare medicinal rohita. Soon after this, the doctor who had recommenced his search was surprised to find what he had been looking for over many previous years. The doctor quickly made a medicine which acted as an effective cure, saving many lives threatened by disease.

As the doctor killed the fish, the fish took the same rebirth over and over again to provide the medicinal substance which would be used to benefit many other beings. In this way King Pemachen was able to cherish and benefit countless sentient beings. King Pemachen was able to give up his physical form, first as a human and then over and over again as a fish, because he regarded others more highly than himself. This was accomplished through the force of love.

The results of King Pemachen's actions finally led him to Buddhahood, perfect Enlightenment. Likewise, we should consider that if we too practise love sincerely, we will produce the same result of attaining Enlightenment. We should make a strong determination to cherish others more than ourself, and as we arise from our meditation on love we should try to retain this wish within our mind.*

THE DISADVANTAGES OF SELF-CHERISHING

The second method of developing the realization of love is seeing the faults and disadvantages of the self-cherishing mind. For countless years we have cherished ourself, caring only for our own welfare in order to try to fulfil our wishes. Over countless aeons we have been trying to achieve happiness in this way, experiencing hardship after hardship, but what actual benefit have we ever received through cherishing ourself ? Instead of experiencing happiness through self-cherishing, this attitude only leads to constant suffering and rebirth in samsara. All the suffering in the universe is created by the self-cherishing mind; our self-cherishing attitude is the basis for all of our suffering. If we really investigate this skilfully, we will establish that it is correct.

It is very important to know that suffering is dependent upon the mind. If there were no feelings, then there would be no suffering. The nature of feeling is the mind. Since feelings do not exist externally but only within the mind, suffering also arises within the mind.

For those who have attained liberation or nirvana, like the Buddhas or the Arhats (Foe Destroyers), there is no further experience of suffering. Although these awakened beings meet with external unfavourable circumstances and conditions of suffering, no matter how extreme these are, they will not experience suffering. These liberated beings do not experience suffering because suffering is entirely dependent upon the

* The benefits of cherishing others are explained more extensively in *Meaningful to Behold* by Geshe Kelsang Gyatso (Wisdom Publications, 1980), a commentary on Shantideva's *Guide to the Bodhisattva's Way of Life*. Shantideva is very clear in this work and explains many methods for training in cherishing others and for cultivating the supreme wish of bodhicitta.

mind, and in their minds the roots of suffering have been eliminated.

Many great meditators have spent most of their lives with very few comforts in the way of material possessions and food, yet their minds remained extremely happy. Milarepa, for example, turned green through having to eat nettles because there was no other source of food available. Despite this, Milarepa's mind remained very content because he had developed an inner happiness which did not depend on external conditions.

Such examples show that true happiness is developed from within. By considering the meditators who developed true inner happiness, the statement that the foundation of suffering is the self-cherishing mind becomes easier to accept. If we have not studied and meditated on the Mahayana teachings in order to know the beneficial results that come about through practising this path, then it will be very difficult to accept this. We should realize that the self-cherishing mind is the source of all our suffering and make a strong determination that from now until we reach Enlightenment we will cherish others more highly than ourself.

In conclusion, we should try to develop the understanding that from beginningless time until the present we have received nothing but suffering as a result of our constant self-cherishing thoughts. Despite all the efforts of our self-cherishing mind, we have been reborn without choice into samsara. We should further reflect that now, having at last come into contact with the Mahayana teachings, if we practise love purely we will eventually attain Enlightenment — the state in which we will no longer experience suffering or pain.

Thinking in this way, developing a positive feeling for achieving the goal of Enlightenment, we should then meditate on this with single-pointed concentration. This is the meditation on love.

Meditation means fixing our mind single-pointedly on any wholesome object. Whatever we are meditating on, it is important to develop a positive feeling toward the object of meditation. This can be achieved, for instance, when meditating on love, by considering the benefits which will come about through the meditation.

The way to meditate on love and the way to meditate on impermanence or emptiness are different, and it is important that this difference should be recognized. When we meditate on impermanence, impermanence is the object while the subject is our mind. We should then try to maintain our full concentration on impermanence and try not to lose mindfulness of this object, remaining on it single-pointedly. The same is true for visualizing Buddha's form. The Buddha's form is the object of meditation, and again our mind is the subject. We should try not to forget the object of meditation and try to keep our mind on it for as long as possible.

In contrast, when we meditate on love we should try to transform our mind into the nature of love. By means of concentration, the subjective mind becomes mixed with its object, love, with the result that there is no gap between the two. In this way we should try to dissolve completely our self-cherishing mind and replace it with the mind of love — cherishing others more than ourself. This is a fundamental point and therefore the difference between these types of meditation should be understood. If we know how to meditate by using the correct method, our meditation becomes very powerful. If we hear a teaching but do not know the correct method to meditate on it, our practice will become difficult and the results of our meditation will be limited.

Whether or not we can practise love immediately is, of course, dependent upon ourself; but it is very important to train in the practice of love toward others, developing love equally for friends, enemies and strangers.

When cultivating love for our enemies, we should consider that enemies are not permanent, but that this kind of relationship often changes. A person whom we regard as an enemy can later become a friend, sharing a deep bond of love. Just as an enemy can change and become a friend or even our husband or wife, it is also possible for a friend to change into an enemy. Seeing these changing circumstances of life — how our friends have often been our enemies and our enemies have been our friends — we should try to develop equal love for all beings. If we can develop love for our enemies, then it is easy to develop love for friends and strangers.

REMEMBERING THE KINDNESS OF OTHERS

The third method of developing the realization of love is to remember the kindness of others. We should consider how we depend on the kindness of others. There are countless examples of how the hard work of others benefits us.

For instance, our food comes to us through the kindness of others. The hard work of the farmers, processors and distributors provides us with food. Our clothes and our house have also been made by the hard work of other people. If we consider our education, our medical treatment, and even our ability to travel by road, rail or plane, all of these benefits come about through the kindness of others.

Even animals are very kind to us and provide us with many benefits. Cows, for example, provide us with milk and sheep give us wool. Many animals even lose their lives so that we may have food and clothing. Without the kindness of others our life would be extremely difficult – if we were able to survive at all.

Just as we receive so much kindness from others in this present life, we have also received kindness in our countless past lives. During the course of our numberless past lives since beginningless time, all beings have acted as our mother, selflessly cherishing and caring for us. By contemplating the kindness of our present mother, the suffering she voluntarily undertook for our sake and the constant love and concern she showed for us, we can understand that all sentient beings – who have acted as our mother in many past lives – have been incredibly kind.

Even if we find it hard to realize that all beings have been our mother, we should consider that they have definitely been very kind to us in past lives. Each being has been our friend and benefactor many times.

In summary, we should remember and contemplate upon the kindness of others which surrounds us in this life. We should also remember that this kindness has likewise benefited us in our previous lives. Remembering the kindness of others, we should try to develop love for all beings.

CHAPTER 11

COMPASSION

The practice of the compassionate mind is very important and helpful to everyone, to religious and non-religious people alike. Even if we cannot conceive of the ultimate benefits of practising the compassionate mind, there are many temporary benefits of compassion. A person who lacks the compassionate mind does not have a good heart.

One day when the great Tibetan yogi Milarepa was meditating in a cave, he heard some noise outside and then saw a large number of wild animals coming toward his cave. Milarepa thought that an enemy must be chasing the animals. A dog belonging to a hunter appeared next and sat down outside Milarepa's cave with the other animals. The wild animals and the hunter's dog became friends. After a short while the hunter arrived. He was extremely surprised to see that his dog, which he had trained to chase and catch other animals, and the wild animals had become friends. The friendship of the dog and the wild animals came about because of Milarepa's blessing. But the hunter thought that Milarepa had used black magic on his dog and he became very angry. He said to Milarepa,

> 'What did you do to my dog? Usually my dog can catch any animal.'

The hunter became still more enraged and said to Milarepa,

> 'I want to kill you!'

Milarepa answered,

> 'You have a human being's form but an animal's mind. Lord Buddha said the human form is very precious; however, human forms like yours are not precious. Your mind and the mind of an animal are the same.'

Thus, Milarepa stated that although people who have no compassion have a human form, they have an animal's mind. Because we have obtained the precious human form it is very important to practise compassion.

The compassionate mind will be explained here in four sections. The first section will give the definition of compassion. The second will outline the benefits of practising the compassionate mind. Next, the objects of the compassionate mind will be discussed. Fourth, the way to practise the compassionate mind will be explained.

THE DEFINITION OF COMPASSION

The compassionate mind is defined as a wholesome thought which wishes others to be released from their sufferings. The compassionate mind wants the sufferings and problems of sentient beings to be relieved. If a member of our family, our father for instance, were ill and we developed a strong desire for him to be freed from his illness, this would be an example of compassion. Or if a friend has problems and we wish him to be relieved of these problems, this is also our compassionate mind.

It is possible that sometimes compassion may be mixed with attachment. When we develop compassion for relatives or friends, sometimes this compassionate mind is also mixed with attachment. Even though this compassionate mind is mixed with the deluded mind of attachment, it is nevertheless important to practise and cultivate compassion for our friends and relatives. At first, if we have no compassion for our friends and relatives, how can we develop a compassionate mind toward other beings? Therefore, developing the compassionate mind which wishes our friends and relatives to be freed from their suffering is a starting point for the development of wider compassion.

If we develop a very powerful wish for all sentient beings to be relieved of their sufferings, this is the mind of great compassion. In the beginning it is very difficult to develop this great compassionate mind for all sentient beings. In order to attain the great compassionate mind we should first practise compassion for a small group of beings, gradually extending this to include all sentient beings.

It is easy to understand that the compassionate mind is the thought which wishes sentient beings to be relieved of their sufferings. But it is not enough to understand the compassionate mind intellectually: at the same time we should try to practise it. To practise the compassionate mind, we generate compassion mentally. In order to meditate on compassion, for instance, it is unnecessary to perform any physical action. The essential thing is to develop compassion in our mind, to turn our mind in a positive direction.

THE BENEFITS OF THE COMPASSIONATE MIND

It is said that there are many benefits to be gained by practising the precious mind of compassion. If we practise the compassionate mind, it helps us to experience happiness and tranquillity and also helps to give tranquillity to the minds of others. The compassionate mind helps to dispel our negative thoughts such as anger, jealousy, etc., and to overcome mental illness. The practice of compassion makes our mind very calm and works to purify our negative actions or negative karma. Meditating upon and practising compassion and bodhicitta has great power to purify negative actions.

If we practise compassion unceasingly it causes others to behave kindly to us. It also leads to rebirth with an attractive form as a human being or to rebirth as a god. Respect or friendship from others will be the result of practising compassion. In addition, there are many other such temporary benefits of practising the compassionate mind.

The ultimate advantages of practising compassion include the rapid development of bodhicitta – the mind of Enlightenment. Someone who practises compassion can also quickly reach other spiritual paths that lead to Enlightenment. Also, when the practitioner of compassion becomes a Buddha, he or she can then benefit others in many ways. After they have attained Enlightenment, Buddhas benefit others because they have great compassionate minds. Without the mind of great compassion one can attain nirvana like the Arhat of the Hinayana tradition. An Arhat has no suffering but lacks the great compassionate impulse to work for the welfare of all universal sentient beings. Buddhas, in contrast, have the precious mind of great compassion and work unceasingly to benefit others. If one possesses the mind of great compassion, one will regard others as more precious than oneself.

The great Mahayana master Chandrakirti said that the mind of great compassion is very important at the beginning, the middle and at the final part of Dharma practice. This means, first, that if one has the mind of great compassion, one can enter into the Mahayana path. Second, through the force of great compassion, one can complete the entire number of spiritual paths of the Mahayana tradition. Third, this means one can work for the sake of all sentient beings after reaching Enlightenment.

It has been said many times that the great compassionate mind is the root of the Mahayana paths and it is also the root of bodhicitta. Therefore, there arise unimaginable benefits from practising this compassionate mind. If we develop a very qualified compassionate mind, this is a precious mind not possessed by many other beings, not even by a high god such as Brahma. A person who generates the mind of great compassion has a very special and valuable mind. If we contemplate the temporary and ultimate benefits of the compassionate mind there will arise a strong desire to practise compassion.

THE OBJECTS OF COMPASSION

All sentient beings are objects of the compassionate mind. No single sentient being is not the object of the compassionate mind because each and every sentient being experiences suffering. All living creatures have sufferings, problems and fears; therefore all these creatures are the objects of compassion. We should extend our compassion to all sentient beings.

It is said that Buddhas and other realized beings are not objects of compassion. The reason for this is that Buddhas do not experience suffering or problems. Thus, we do not need to meditate on compassion for the Buddhas; instead we should meditate on compassion for all sentient beings. It is sometimes possible that a sentient being may feel compassionate toward a Buddha. But is that real compassion? There is one story which illustrates this point.

On the bank of the River Ganges there was an old woman who had leprosy and was in very poor condition. A monk called Kusali met the old woman who was, in fact, an emanation of Vajrayogini, a female Enlightened being. In order to protect the monk, Vajrayogini manifested herself as a poor-looking old woman. The monk Kusali felt strong compassion when he met the old woman and asked her where she was going. The old woman replied,

> 'I would like to cross the River Ganges, but I have been on this bank for many days and no one has helped me. Therefore, I need assistance.'

The monk developed a very strong compassionate mind and said,

> 'Get on my back and I will take you across.'

With the old woman on his back, the monk started to cross the River Ganges. When he reached the middle of the river, the old woman transformed into Vajrayogini. Buddha Vajrayogini then took the monk to her pure land.

In this story the person who felt compassion was an ordinary being and the object of compassion was a Buddha. But when the monk developed compassion for the old woman, he did not realize that the object of his compassion was an emanation of Vajrayogini, not a poor sentient being. He did not consciously feel compassion for a Buddha. If we do realize that the object is a Buddha, and then we develop compassion, this is mistaken compassion. But the monk in the story did not know the object of his compassionate mind was a Buddha instead of an old woman; therefore his compassion was not mistaken. But in general the objects of our compassion are all sentient beings.

HOW TO PRACTISE THE COMPASSIONATE MIND

The practice of the compassionate mind will be explained here for people who are not very familiar with the Buddhist teachings. First, we should try to develop a compassionate mind toward our friends and relatives. This is an easier kind of compassion to practise and it should be followed by developing wider compassion. To cultivate compassion for our close friends and relatives, we should consider the kinds of suffering they experience. We might think that they experience little suffering, but according to Dharma this is not the case. If we think carefully we can see that even if they are not experiencing great suffering now, in the future they will experience inevitable sufferings such as sickness, old age and death. Our friends and relatives have no choice: because they took samsaric rebirth they will experience suffering.

After considering the sufferings to which those close to us are subject, we should think,

> 'How wonderful it would be if they were released from samsaric suffering!'

If we can generate this thought or feeling we should hold on to it without letting it diminish. We should meditate on this compassionate thought. When this thought arises our mind has been transformed into the precious mind of compassion. Even when we are not in meditation we should not forget this compassionate attitude.

What will be the effects of generating a compassionate mind and practising compassion every day? We will develop a very wholesome mind and this will lead to good relationships with others. By contemplating every day upon others' unhappiness, problems and sufferings, we will feel a responsibility to try and relieve their sufferings.

Also, it is important to think that because we have received Dharma teachings we should practise compassion. Although our friends may not have received Dharma teachings on the compassionate mind, we have been fortunate enough to have received the teachings, and therefore we can put them into practice. Others who have not received the teachings will not have the same opportunity to generate a compassionate mind.

The practice of compassion is very helpful in day-to-day life. If we successfully develop compassion for our friends and relatives, we should then extend this to others. Through contemplating the sufferings of our neighbours, fellow citizens, people in hospitals and prisons, we can gain an understanding of how others experience suffering.

When farmers observe the lives of office workers they may think that such people have a very good life. But even office workers have no pure happiness; rather they have many worries and inner and outer problems. When the office workers consider the farmers, they may think that farmers have a very pleasant life. But farmers have to work hard every day and have many hardships. The office workers may consider that presidents and prime ministers have a happy life, but they too have no pure happiness. They can have more mental problems, more dangers and more fears than other people. If we examine different life situations carefully, we can see that everyone has suffering.

What is the basic cause of everyone's suffering? The cause is rebirth in samsara or cyclic existence. The source of all our problems is our impure rebirth. Realizing that all beings born into samsara have many problems, we should think:

'How excellent it would be if all beings were free from their inner problems!'

This feeling or thought is the compassionate mind which we should try to develop and hold or concentrate upon.

Sometimes we may find it difficult to generate compassion for those who are very rich, hold high positions, or are more fortunate than ourself. But it is also possible to develop compassion for these people. Compassion can be developed on the basis of realizing the future sufferings of people who are now fortunate. We can feel compassion for the wealthy person who, although not appearing to suffer now, will definitely experience sufferings such as sickness and death in the future. No one holds a high position permanently. Buddha said that whoever has high rank finally loses it. In samsara there is not one being who never falls from higher to lower status. Thus, the rich and powerful will one day lose their privileged positions.

We should think that a person who experiences great suffering now and a rich or highly placed person who is not now experiencing great suffering are really the same. One person experiences suffering now; the other will experience suffering in the future. Both are equal in their experience of suffering; the difference is only the time during which the suffering occurs. Thinking in this way, we should try to cultivate a compassionate mind toward the wealthy and powerful.

Sometimes it is difficult to develop a compassionate mind for our enemies. We should consider that even though an enemy tried to harm us, he experienced terrible suffering through developing an angry mind. By harming us the enemy lost his mental peace and happiness. Seeing in this way the enemy had no choice but was forced by delusion to act against us, we can try to develop compassion for our enemies. Without contemplating the sufferings of our enemies and their lack of freedom when they are motivated by negative conceptual thoughts, it is difficult to feel compassion for them. But if we practise skilfully we can develop a compassionate mind toward all sentient beings; however, without training ourself this is hard to do.

After we have developed compassion for all human beings by contemplating the many sufferings which all humans experience, we should extend our compassion to animals. If we think, for instance, of the cows which are slaughtered by human beings, we will feel compassion for their sufferings. The cows which are now peacefully grazing in fields will soon be taken to the slaughterhouse. If we contemplate this we can feel compassion for these animals. In a similar way, by contemplating the sufferings of other animals we can develop compassion for them.

There is another method of generating the mind of great compassion. First, we should contemplate our own problems and sufferings. We should consider our mental or inner problems, physical problems, and problems of gaining and keeping possessions. Future sufferings and sufferings of all other kinds should be contemplated. Obviously, we will experience the sufferings of sickness, old age and death. In between these problems, many more problems will arise. Our next life will bring still more problems because ordinary beings have no choice about when or where they take rebirth. In summary, we should think that we have no real choice but must encounter much pain, great suffering, and many problems in the future. By contemplating our own suffering there will arise a wish to escape from it. This wish or thought is renunciation; but it is not the mind of compassion.

If we develop the strong feeling of having many, many problems and sufferings, we should then consider that all other beings experience equal amounts of suffering. We should think:

'No matter how much I suffer, I am only one individual; but others are of infinite number. How wonderful it would be if all these numberless beings were relieved of their sufferings!'

Shantideva said that first we should contemplate our own problems and then, taking these as an example, try to develop compassion for all other beings.

If we cannot first develop the wish to escape from the sufferings of cyclic existence, it is very difficult to develop the wish for others to be separated from their sufferings in cyclic existence. Sometimes it is hard to develop a desire to avoid our sufferings because we cannot recognize them. We fail to understand that cyclic existence is full of sufferings. But if we can recognize our own sufferings, we should develop the wish to escape from them. Then, changing the object of our thinking, we should cultivate the wish for all others to be released from their many sufferings. This last wish is the mind of great compassion. Thus, practising this method helps to develop the mind of great compassion.

Je Tsong Khapa said that there are two principal methods to develop great compassion. The first one is to practise and meditate mainly upon affectionate love for all sentient beings. The second method is upon the basis of affectionate love, if we mainly contemplate others' sufferings, the mind of great compassion will arise. If we have successfully meditated on affectionate love and contemplated the sufferings of others, the mind of great compassion can be gained easily.

Buddhists talk about suffering for many reasons. No one really likes to hear about suffering or wishes to experience it, but by contemplating suffering we can reach spiritual realizations. For spiritual development it is necessary to see the faults of samsara; therefore we should meditate

on suffering again and again. Through contemplating our own suffering we can develop renunciation; through contemplating the suffering of others we can develop the mind of great compassion. Contemplating suffering in these ways leads us to great benefits.

Three types of suffering

All sentient beings experience three types of suffering: the suffering of misery, the suffering of change, and pervasive suffering. The first type, the suffering of misery, comprises physical sufferings such as pain, old age and death, and mental anxieties. This kind of suffering is familiar and is not difficult to recognize.

The latter two sufferings, the suffering of change and pervasive suffering, are more difficult to understand as being suffering. Because these two kinds of suffering are not usually recognized as being suffering, many beings consider that they are happy in their samsaric existence. But it is important to realize that these two kinds of suffering exist.

The suffering of change is apparent happiness which is developed through the force of reducing great suffering. But soon this apparent happiness transforms into suffering. For example, if we are extremely hungry, when we eat some food at first we experience apparent happiness. But in reality such apparent happiness is the suffering of change: we have only reduced our great suffering. If we eat more and more, soon eating will become a cause of suffering. In the same way all samsaric happinesses are of the nature of the suffering of change.

The samsaric body and mind are pervasive suffering. The reason for this is that all suffering arises from the samsaric body or mind. Pervasive suffering is like the ocean from which different types of suffering arise like waves.

Every sentient being experiences these three sufferings. If we visualize all sentient beings surrounding us and experiencing endless suffering, we will wish them to be free from their sufferings. If we concentrate on these countless sentient beings, we will receive benefits equal to the number of beings visualized.

If we can recognize the three types of suffering and develop compassion for all sentient beings, this is excellent. But if we cannot do this at the moment we should begin now to train or cultivate a compassionate mind. It is very important to contemplate and meditate on the compassionate mind. The teachings about the compassionate mind are not very hard to understand. But it is difficult to develop and gain experience of the compassionate mind without exerting great effort. Therefore, we need to direct our efforts and energies toward achieving the mind of compassion.

CHAPTER 12

THE ALTRUISTIC MIND OF ENLIGHTENMENT

In order to develop bodhicitta, the altruistic mind of Enlightenment, we must have the motivation of great compassion. With the motivation of great compassion, we can develop the strong wish to attain Enlightenment for the sake of others. This spontaneous wish to achieve Enlightenment for the sake of all other sentient beings is bodhicitta. The mind of bodhicitta finds it very difficult to bear the sufferings of others and wishes to dispel their sufferings by gaining Enlightenment.

A father who has many children will feel responsibility for his children's sufferings. He will find the sufferings of his children hard to bear. To enable him to relieve his children's sufferings and problems, the father works hard and wishes to earn more money. He thinks that without more money he cannot alleviate their sufferings. The Bodhisattva, in a similar way, finds it difficult to bear the sufferings of every sentient being. In order to relieve others' sufferings the Bodhisattva thinks that he or she must attain Enlightenment.

It is this precious mind of the Bodhisattva — bodhicitta — that we should develop. But without training our mind bodhicitta will never arise automatically. Although some people, because of their imprints from past lives, can develop bodhicitta quite easily, in general we must train our mind rigorously in order to cultivate bodhicitta.

It is said that the mind of bodhicitta is the most precious and most sublime mind of realized beings; it is the most excellent type of mind. Atisha, for example, had great knowledge in many fields; he also had many attainments such as clairvoyance, miracle powers, and the realization of emptiness. He was very skilful in both Sutra and Tantra and in the inner signs of religion. Although Atisha had all this vast knowledge, he considered bodhicitta to be unsurpassable. Atisha never regarded his clairvoyance or miracle powers very highly, whereas he regarded bodhicitta as his most precious attainment.

Atisha had many teachers or gurus. He regarded the guru who gave him instructions about bodhicitta as his most precious teacher. Atisha himself was a very experienced teacher. The Tibetans invited him to Tibet and he gave there many teachings about both Sutra and Tantra.

When Atisha was in Tibet he used to hear the names of his teachers in India. When he heard the name of his teacher Serlingpa who had taught him about bodhicitta, he would cry, bow and make prostrations. For his other teachers' names he would not do this. When the Tibetans asked Atisha why he had special respect and devotion for Serlingpa, he explained that his teachers were very kind to him, but among his teachers the most precious and kindest one was Serlingpa, the teacher of bodhicitta. From other teachers Atisha received many other teachings and Tantric empowerments, but Lama Serlingpa was regarded by Atisha as the most precious of all his teachers.

There are many different levels of bodhicitta, but all of these can be divided into two: the aspiring mind of bodhicitta and the venturing or engaging mind of bodhicitta. The aspiring mind of bodhicitta is the desire or wish to attain Enlightenment for the welfare of others. It is like the wish to go to London without actually preparing for the journey or starting out. The engaging mind of bodhicitta, in contrast, is not satisfied with merely wishing to reach Enlightenment for the benefit of others; it actually enters into the special paths that lead to Enlightenment. If someone who has the aspiring mind of bodhicitta takes the Bodhisattva vows and then engages in practices such as generosity, patience, moral discipline, joyous effort, concentration and wisdom, this person has the engaging mind of bodhicitta. The engaging mind of bodhicitta is like having the wish to go to London and then in fact going.

We must first develop the aspiring mind of bodhicitta. We all have many wishes such as wanting friends, money, a house, etc., but we rarely consider the desire to reach Enlightenment. However, if we contemplate the benefits of the altruistic mind of Enlightenment, this will become the cause of developing bodhicitta.

THE BENEFITS OF BODHICITTA

The Buddhist texts of both Sutra and Tantra explain the benefits of developing bodhicitta. These extensive benefits are summarized in the following ten main types of benefits.

The first benefit is that bodhicitta is the gateway to the Mahayana paths. Just as it is necessary to go in through the door if we wish to enter a room, it is necessary to develop the precious altruistic mind of Enlightenment in order to become a Mahayana yogi or yogini. Merely reading a book about the Mahayana path is not enough: we must practise bodhicitta. Without the motivation of bodhicitta the advanced practices of the Mahayana Sutras and Secret Mantra will never become real Mahayana practices.

Second, a person who is generating bodhicitta becomes a son or daughter of the Buddhas. He or she becomes a part of the family of the Buddhas. This is beneficial because once one has entered the family of the Buddhas by cultivating bodhicitta, one will soon become a Buddha.

The third benefit of bodhicitta is that one can surpass the realized beings of the Hinayana path. In general, Hinayana yogis such as Arhats are very highly realized beings because they have abandoned deluded minds. They can maintain mental peace and therefore, compared to ordinary beings, they are highly realized. But by attaining the precious mind of bodhicitta one can surpass the Arhats and other realized Hinayana practitioners because they do not possess the mind of bodhicitta. In the same way that a very young prince or princess is of higher rank than the high government ministers, someone who has developed the mind of bodhicitta surpasses the highly realized beings of the Hinayana path.

The fourth benefit is that if one has the mind of bodhicitta, one becomes the object of veneration and offerings from others. No matter what a person's external appearance or social position may be, someone who develops the altruistic mind of bodhicitta becomes worthy of the veneration of humans and worldly gods such as Brahma and Indra.

Fifth, a person who has bodhicitta can complete the two accumulations very quickly. The two accumulations of merit and wisdom enable one to attain Enlightenment. The complete accumulation of meritorious power or merit leads to the achievement of a Buddha's divine body and the full accumulation of wisdom enables one to attain a Buddha's divine mind.

The sixth benefit of cultivating the precious mind of bodhicitta is that it purifies the very strong negative mental imprints or karma that one has amassed. There are many true stories about the power of bodhicitta to purify negative karma.

The fulfilment of all one's wishes is the seventh benefit of bodhicitta. This means that if one wishes to escape from the sufferings of cyclic existence and to free others from these sufferings, bodhicitta can accomplish this. Through the force of bodhicitta, oneself and all other sentient beings will be able to experience pure and immeasurable happiness without end.

The eighth benefit of bodhicitta is that others, such as non-human beings, spirits, and the four external elements – earth, water, fire and air – will not harm the possessor of bodhicitta. Since the elements, non-human beings and spirits cannot harm him or her, the possessor of bodhicitta has no reason to feel afraid. A person who posesses the mind of bodhicitta, a Bodhisattva, has no fear because of cherishing others more than himself or herself. Bodhisattvas regard others as mothers regard their children. Thus, when someone tries to harm a Bodhisattva, the Bodhisattva never feels fear; instead he or she develops love. For these reasons, if we develop bodhicitta we will be free from fears.

The ninth benefit of developing bodhicitta is that the five Mahayana paths and the ten spiritual grounds of the Arya Bodhisattvas will soon be completed. The Bodhisattva must traverse these paths and grounds in order to reach Enlightenment. For example, if we wish to go from York to London by train we must pass certain stations on the way. Likewise, if we wish to reach Enlightenment we must pass ten stations on the way. These are not railway stations, but rather the ten spiritual grounds of the Aryas. After reaching the tenth ground Buddhahood will be attained.

Finally, the tenth benefit of bodhicitta is that the possessor of bodhicitta will gain Enlightenment speedily. Everyone who has attained the state of full Enlightenment has done so by developing the precious altruistic mind of Enlightenment. Therefore we should direct our energies toward developing bodhicitta in order to attain Enlightenment quickly.

These are the concise ten benefits of developing bodhicitta. If we think about the ten benefits again and again, this practice is called analytical meditation. By doing this analytical meditation we will develop the motivation to attain the mind of bodhicitta. Just as when we consider the profits of doing business, the more we consider the profits, the more effort we put into the business. Equally, if we see the benefits of developing bodhicitta, we will wish to generate this precious mind and we will exert great effort to achieve this goal.

HOW TO DEVELOP BODHICITTA: A CONCISE EXPLANATION

There are three methods for developing bodhicitta: through the force of the six causes, through the force of equalizing and exchanging oneself with others, and through the force of the four causes or conditions. The first two methods exist because the Buddha passed on two different lineages of developing the mind of bodhicitta. The first lineage comes from the teachings Shakyamuni Buddha gave to Maitreya, who passed the lineage to Asanga. Asanga passed the lineage on to Vasubandhu, who passed it on in an unbroken lineage up to our teachers. The lineage of the second method is based on the teachings the Buddha expounded to Manjushri, who passed the instructions on to Shantideva. Shantideva passed on the lineage in unbroken form to many other teachers and the lineage remains unbroken up to the present.

The first lineage, the method of developing bodhicitta through the force of the six causes, is easier than the method of exchanging oneself with others. But the latter method is more profound and more powerful. For those of weak mind, exchanging oneself with others is very difficult to practise. If someone has little wisdom and no teacher, the method of exchanging oneself with others is troublesome. But for a person who has great wisdom this second method has advantages.

The general technique for cultivating bodhicitta is through the force of the six causes. The first of these causes is to recognize all sentient beings as having been one's mother. The second cause is remembering the kindness of all these sentient beings. The third cause is wishing to repay the kindness of all sentient beings who have been one's mother. Developing affectionate love for all beings is the fourth cause. The fifth cause is developing great compassion. The last of the six causes is the superior intention. The effect of these six causes is that one will gain the precious mind of bodhicitta. The six causes will not be explained here; for more details about how to meditate on and practise the six causes, the reader should consult other works.*

The four causes

Another method to develop the mind of Enlightenment or bodhicitta is through the force of four causes. The first cause is to know and remember the benefits of becoming a Buddha and the powers of a

*See, for example, *Meaningful to Behold* by Geshe Kelsang Gyatso.

Buddha. We should study and remember that a Buddha is endowed with clairvoyance, miracle powers and all physical, verbal and mental excellences. If we know the excellences of a Buddha and the powers and benefits of a Buddha, there will arise a strong desire to become a Buddha ourself because a Buddha is free from all fears, has skilful means to benefit others, and has many extraordinary powers. A Buddha's actions and powers are beyond analogy and beyond our comprehension. There is no higher being than a Buddha. Therefore we should think:

'How wonderful it would be if I, myself, became a Buddha!'

The second cause for developing bodhicitta derives from not being able to bear the disappearance of the Mahayana teachings. That is, we realize that if the Mahayana teachings disappear there is no possibility of reaching Enlightenment. These teachings were expounded by Shakyamuni Buddha to enable others to attain Buddhahood. Previously the Mahayana teachings flourished in many Eastern countries, but today they have become very rare.

How do we know that the Mahayana teachings are so rare? The attitudes and practices of the Mahayanist are those of higher beings such as Bodhisattvas. It is very difficult for ordinary beings to accept these Mahayana practices. Therefore most ordinary beings will abandon the Mahayana teachings; some people may even criticize these teachings. Also, it is extremely difficult to find a qualified Mahayana teacher. Followers of the Mahayana teachings are also very few. For these reasons pure Mahayana teachings are rare.

There is a great danger that the Mahayana teachings in this world will be extinguished; then there will be no way for beings on this earth to reach a Buddha's supreme state. Therefore, before the Mahayana teachings disappear we should think that we need to reach Enlightenment for the sake of others and we should take this valuable opportunity to practise the Mahayana teachings intensively. In this way we should try to become a Buddha as soon as possible, while we still have the Mahayana teachings to guide us to Enlightenment.

The third cause is to remember that if we do not become a Buddha many beings will experience unbearable sufferings. In order to relieve their sufferings we should wish to attain Enlightenment. Only an Enlightened being, a Buddha, has the power to help suffering beings in many ways. Thus, the thought of relieving others' sufferings and the resulting wish to achieve Enlightenment are the third cause of bodhicitta. If we develop the third cause, then we actually develop bodhicitta. If we cannot bear to have others suffer we will experience the desire to gain Enlightenment. This is the true bodhicitta.

The fourth cause is that we should reflect that we have met the Mahayana teachings and a Mahayana teacher and therefore we have a great opportunity to achieve Buddhahood. While we have the Mahayana teacher and teachings we should cultivate a strong wish to reach Buddhahood at once. We should develop the precious mind of bodhicitta by thinking continuously about these four causes.

Overcoming doubts

Sometimes we may develop negative doubts such as wondering how Enlightenment can be attained because we can't understand how Buddhas can exist. If this happens we should contemplate the reasons for the existence of Buddhas by means of the scriptures and by means of reasoning. At times we may feel that Buddha is very far away and then become discouraged because a Buddha's mind is so perfect whereas our own mind is extremely imperfect. Therefore we doubt whether Enlightenment can be achieved.

But there is no point in becoming discouraged. If we have strong joyous effort and strong energy for practising Dharma, we can become a Buddha because we have the opportunity to practise all of the path that leads to Enlightenment. We have met a Dharma teacher and received Dharma teachings. Negative powers are not permanent – they soon change. If we exert great effort all things can be changed. The Buddha said that all sentient beings will reach Buddhahood. This means that all sentient beings including insects have the Buddha nature or Buddha seed within them. Because we are human we can practise all of the profound methods to achieve Enlightenment. If we have all of these favourable conditions and we exercise great effort, we can certainly attain Buddha's supreme Enlightened state. In this way we should encourage and uplift our mind.

Sometimes it is beneficial to read the stories and biographies of the spiritual teachers of the past who attained Buddhahood, including Shakyamuni Buddha. Tibet was a country with a small population compared to other countries, but there were many Dharma practitioners there who became Enlightened in just one lifetime. Also in India and in other countries many people reached Enlightenment. Therefore, if we have strong joyous effort, what can prevent us too from becoming a Buddha?

At the very beginning Shakyamuni Buddha was not a Buddha; he was just as we are now — very ordinary. Then, through the force of his joyous effort he trained in the spiritual paths and became Enlightened. If Shakyamuni Buddha had not shown this path for reaching Enlightenment we would have no path to Buddhahood. But because he showed us the entirety of the path to Enlightenment we have a clear path to follow. It is very important to cultivate the wish to become Enlightened and then practise Dharma with great effort in order to attain this goal.

At the moment we have two kinds of obscurations. One is the obscurations preventing liberation; the other is the obscurations preventing omniscience. The obscurations preventing liberation include all of our negative minds such as anger, greed, pride, jealousy, envy and so forth. The obscurations preventing omniscience are the imprints of these deluded minds.

Our mind is now overcast by these two types of obscurations. These obscurations are like clouds which cover the pure, lucid sky of our mind. There is, however, a method or remedy to dispel the two cloud-like obscurations. The method is to train in the Mahayana teachings. By practising the Mahayana teachings we are able to clear away the two obscurations. Our mind then becomes completely pure, like a cloudless sky. When we reach this stage of having a clear, pure, unobstructed mind, we have become a Buddha. While we have the two obscurations we are a sentient being; when we become free from the obscurations we become a Buddha or Enlightened being.

We can know that we have the potentiality to become free from these obscurations by seeing that the obscurations are not permanent, but constantly changing. We can also reflect that the two obscurations have antidotes which weaken their power. Thus the more we practise the antidotes, the weaker the obscurations become, until finally they disappear. For these reasons we should not doubt the existence of Buddhas, fully Enlightened beings, nor should we doubt that individuals like ourself can achieve Enlightenment.

CHAPTER 13

EMPTINESS

The study and practice of emptiness are profound and vast, and in Tibet students studied emptiness over a period of many years. The explanation of emptiness presented here will be only a brief outline.

It is very important to understand what is meant by 'emptiness'. It is also important to internalize emptiness, to know it through our own experience. In order to experience emptiness – the true nature of phenomena – it must first be understood intellectually. If we do not first understand emptiness intellectually, it will be very difficult actually to gain experience of emptiness. Understanding emptiness on an intellectual level is the preparation for the intuitive realization of emptiness to develop. Thus, there are two ways to understand emptiness: intellectually and through our own experience.

HOW TO UNDERSTAND EMPTINESS INTELLECTUALLY

When we first investigate emptiness we need to know the purpose and the reasons for doing so, the benefits that come about through realizing emptiness, and the faults that arise from not realizing emptiness. If we understand the purpose and benefits of realizing emptiness, we will then acquire a strong aspiring mind which works toward this realization.

Acting out of ignorance of the true nature of reality because we have not realized emptiness, we are constantly creating negative karma. As a result we have to experience endlessly the suffering produced by our negative actions. It was for this reason that the Buddha said the cause of sentient beings experiencing dissatisfaction and suffering in cyclic existence is that they have not realized emptiness.

The root of all our suffering and misery is self-grasping. As long as this wrong conception of self remains present in our mind-stream, we will remain trapped in cyclic existence or samsara. The unsurpassable method for eradicating self-grasping and thereby suffering is the profound view of emptiness.

According to the Buddhist teachings, two main results can be achieved by practising Dharma. The first result is self-liberation from suffering. The second or ultimate result is final Enlightenment — Buddhahood. Without the realization of emptiness it is impossible to reach and experience either of these two states.

Even within the Hinayana tradition of Buddhism, where the emphasis is on self-liberation alone, there is no way to achieve liberation other than by realizing emptiness. In the Mahayana tradition, one seeks full Enlightenment or Buddhahood in order to benefit others. Before attaining final Enlightenment, which is achieved through the practice of the Mahayana path, emptiness must be realized. The attainment of the omniscient Buddha mind depends on the realization of emptiness.

In our daily lives most of us try to solve our problems by external means. Concentrating on our problems in this way can at most be of temporary benefit to us during this present short lifetime. If, however, we were to realize emptiness, concentrating our effort inwardly to do so, we would experience lasting benefits. The realization of emptiness would eradicate all our mental problems and sufferings.

As has been explained earlier, all problems and sufferings depend upon the mind. It is realizing emptiness which destroys our fears and can end the samsaric suffering of our life. When we experience emptiness we can solve all of our problems. Because higher Bodhisattvas have realized emptiness, even if their bodies are cut into small pieces they will feel no pain.

Through the force of realizing emptiness, all temporal problems and miseries are overcome and ultimately we obtain pure and everlasting freedom from suffering and pain. At present we must experience uncontrolled suffering in our life because we lack the realization of emptiness. From our own experiences we can see that from the greatest kings, to those in positions of power and wealth, down to the most wretched, all beings suffer from anxieties and frustrations and all beings are without pure freedom. No one wishes to experience the sufferings of sickness, old age and death; yet these befall us naturally. Over these sufferings we have no control.

Some people dislike teachings on emptiness because emptiness and usual appearances are very different. Also, emptiness is extremely subtle and therefore, for some people, it is very difficult to understand. After his Enlightenment the Buddha said,

> 'I have found Dharma which is very much like ambrosia.
> However, the ambrosia-like Dharma is not comprehensible
> to everyone because it is so profound.'

Although emptiness is generally difficult to accept and understand, if in our past lives we have created wholesome mental tendencies and perhaps developed familiarity with aspects of emptiness, emptiness can then of course be realized much more easily. But if we misunderstand emptiness it may disturb our other spiritual practices. There is one particular story which illustrates this point well, showing the danger of misunderstanding the concept of emptiness.

Many years ago there was a Buddhist master who had achieved great fame through his realization of emptiness. He had realized emptiness intuitively and because of this he was invited by a king to become his teacher. The king followed the Buddhist master's teachings on the true nature of phenomena — emptiness. Although the Buddhist master taught the true emptiness, the king developed a misunderstanding owing to the subtleties of the subject matter.

The king began to feel that the master was holding wrong views. He thought that the Buddhist master was saying that nothing existed at all, and thus if he were allowed to continue to give such false teachings to the king's subjects, he would be leading many people in the wrong direction and destroying their spiritual lives. Through this reasoning the king had the master killed.

After some years the king began to follow the instructions of another teacher. But this time the king was not taught emptiness at the very beginning of his practice. First he received teachings on impermanence, the faults of cyclic existence, and the nature of dissatisfaction and suffering. By first explaining subtle impermanence and other basic Dharma teachings, the second teacher caused the king's wisdom to increase. By teaching in this way, when the second teacher finally imparted the teachings on emptiness, no misunderstanding developed. The king eventually attained the realization of emptiness, and through his intuitive understanding was able to see that this emptiness was exactly the same as the emptiness the first teacher had taught. The king, upon realizing this, was filled with deep remorse for having needlessly destroyed the life of his first teacher, the realized master.

Even by reading this chapter some people may misunderstand the meaning of emptiness. At first it is quite possible for hesitations and doubts about emptiness to arise, but if we study continuously the teachings will become very clear. Despite the fact that misunderstandings sometimes develop, it is important to receive teachings about emptiness. It is also important to understand the purpose of studying emptiness and the benefits which come about through studying and realizing emptiness. It is through realizing emptiness that true freedom from suffering and dissatisfaction can be attained.

What is emptiness?

Emptiness is the fact that all phenomena lack inherent existence. In order to understand emptiness we have to use lines of reasoning and examples such as those taught by the Buddha. Without reasons and examples it would be extremely difficult to understand emptiness; therefore we have to rely primarily upon these.

All emptinesses can be divided into two kinds: emptiness of persons and emptiness of other phenomena. The emptiness of a person is the person's lack of inherent existence; the emptiness of a phenomenon is the lack of inherent existence of any phenomenon which is not a person.

Initially, when studying emptiness we should contemplate how a person is empty of inherent existence. A person has two natures – ultimate and conventional. Let us now examine this with the aid of an example. Our example will be a person called John. John has two natures: one is his ultimate nature and the other is his conventional nature. The emptiness of inherent existence is John's ultimate nature; John is of the nature of conventional truth.

When we know the nature of conventional truth, this helps us to understand the nature of ultimate truth. The basis for imputing 'John' is the collection of John's five aggregates. John is composed of the aggregates of form, feeling, discernment, compositional factors and consciousness. The collection of these five aggregates which constitute the person's body and mind is the basis for imputing John. If these five aggregates are not assembled together, there is no basis for imputing John. John, thus, is an imputed phenomenon dependent upon his five aggregates.

If we investigate, we cannot find John among the aggregates of form, feeling, discernment, compositional factors or consciousness. Having in this way established that the five aggregates individually are not the real John, we must then also determine that the collection of the aggregates cannot be John either. This we can do by realizing that since there is not a single thing that is John in the collection of his aggregates, it is impossible for the collection of all these non-John things to be John.

Once we clearly understand that John cannot be found either as any one aggregate nor as the collection of the five aggregates, we must then ask whether it is possible for John to exist outside of or other than this? Since John is imputed on the basis of the five aggregates, it would be impossible for John to exist other than within his five aggregates individually or as a group. By using such methods of logical reasoning, checking precisely, John becomes unfindable and is shown unable inherently to exist. We should now contemplate what this indicates — namely, the fact that after search and investigation John cannot be seen to exist inherently.

We will then discover that John is only imputed by conceptual thought, this being the nature of conventional truth. John, therefore, lacks any inherent existence. 'John' is simply a label imputed by conceptual thought. In summary, John becomes unfindable when we investigate, indicating that he lacks any form of inherent or self-existence. John is nothing more than a phenomenon in the category of persons imputed by a conceptualizing mind.

If John were actually to exist from his own side as an independent entity, then through investigation it would be possible to establish his inherent existence. However, this is not the case and we cannot find an inherently or independently existing John. Therefore we must conclude this investigation by accepting that it is not possible for John inherently to exist. Although this form of logical reasoning may seem repetitive and rigorous at first glance, it is necessary to avoid some of the difficulties in establishing the existence of emptiness.

If the collection of John's five aggregates is John, then among this collection one of the aggregates must be John. For example, if we have a rosary made of one hundred beads, if the collection of one hundred beads is the rosary, then one of these beads or some of them must be the rosary. But this is not the case. Therefore, the mere collection of one hundred beads is not the rosary. Likewise, the mere collection of John's five aggregates is not John because no one of these five aggregates is John.

We should contemplate this example and this reasoning for a long time, considering whether the meaning and the example correspond. Perhaps when we first read this example we may find that it seems totally meaningless. But if we investigate it for a long time, we will find deep meaning.

In the *Middle Way* texts some further lines of logical reasoning are explained as methods to understand emptiness. For instance, if the mere collection of the five aggregates of John is John, then it follows that the mere collection of the parts of a car is a car. If the collection of parts of a car is a car, then it follows that a heap of the parts of a car lying on the ground is a car.

For people who have studied emptiness extensively there will be little doubt about what is being said; however, some people will still believe that the mere collection of the five aggregates, as in the example of John, is actually John. Even some lower Buddhist schools of thought hold this belief. According to the highest Buddhist school, the Prasangika, which embodies the ultimate view of the Buddha, it is never accepted that John is merely the collection of his five aggregates, nor is it accepted that any one of his five aggregates is John. This point is very important to know in order not to misunderstand the teachings on emptiness. Even if the instructor or teacher explains emptiness correctly and clearly, the listener may still misunderstand what has been said. Therefore we need to receive teachings on emptiness from a qualified teacher; we also need to study, contemplate and meditate more upon emptiness in order to understand its subtle nature.

We should investigate what faults or mistakes there are in believing that John's five aggregates are John. If there is absolutely no doubt that the collection of his five aggregates is John, then of course there is no mistake in stating this. However, if we examine precisely, believing that John is the collection of his five aggregates definitely has many logical faults. We should train in these methods of reasoning which will help us to gain an understanding of emptiness. If possible, we should also use examples relating to our own experiences.

HOW TO UNDERSTAND EMPTINESS THROUGH ONE'S OWN EXPERIENCE

Je Tsong Khapa explained some examples such as dreams, illusions, and mistaking a coiled striped rope for a snake to help us to gain insight into emptiness. If we use our own dreams as examples, our understanding of emptiness will become experiential.

Let us consider that last night we dreamt we were climbing on a high mountain. In our dream the mountain was experienced as being real.

Yet how is it possible for the mountain to exist? Such a huge mountain could not exist in our room — it is far too large. Nor is the mountain in the outside world. If we investigate carefully in this way, the mountain is unfindable, indicating that it lacks any inherent existence.

Even though emptiness is very subtle, through the use of lifelike examples such as our dream, it is possible to understand that the mountain, person or whatever we may consider lacks any identity which exists inherently. As another example, we may watch a late-night horror movie based on the appearance of a terrifying monster. When watching the film we experience anxiety and fear. At the time this experience occurs we should ask what it is that we actually fear?

The fear that we experience is caused by the monster which appears to be alive on our television screen. If we investigate precisely, we begin to discover that from its own side or nature the monster does not actually exist. Neither within the television, outside of the television, nor in our house can the monster be found. The monster that we feared has no independent identity or self-existence. Our apprehension of the monster is simply the imputation of conceptual thought. In this same way, we should consider the identity or 'I' which appears to exist independently within ourself.

If we consider the nature of our own identity carefully, the 'I' which exists within ourself — like the identity of the television monster — is not truly existing from its own side. By examining the 'I', we can gain some understanding and personal experience of emptiness. Realizing the emptiness of the 'I' is very different from the way we usually consider ourself to exist.

For those who have faith in the Buddha, the scriptures or teachings of the Buddha are a sufficient cause for them to accept emptiness and to study extensively in order to realize its true meaning. It is said that for those who are unfortunate it will be difficult to realize emptiness. But for those who have created fortunate causes, emptiness can be realized easily. Just as precious jewels are hard to find, they are easy to lose. Likewise, a person who has created the fortunate karma to realize emptiness can easily lose the opportunity to do so. In worldly terms those who are wealthy are fortunate; but in order to reach the profound realization of emptiness we need to accumulate the spiritual fortune of meritorious power.

For people who create evil actions it becomes increasingly difficult to realize emptiness. Just as crops cannot be easily cultivated on rocky ground, it is difficult to cultivate the realization of emptiness within the mind of evil. For this reason the purification of our obstacles and evil actions is of great importance: engaging in such practices is a method through which we can realize emptiness.

If we follow and rely upon Manjushri, the embodiment of all the Buddhas' wisdom, our wisdom will increase and we will not find it difficult to realize emptiness. There are three main practices to actualize emptiness: (1) purifying negative actions, together with accumulating merit, (2) following a very qualified and experienced teacher, and (3) engaging in the actual meditation on emptiness and training through the force of our effort. By engaging in these practices it is possible to gain the experience of emptiness whereas without these practices, gaining the experience of emptiness is extremely difficult.

In order to understand emptiness it is important to know that all phenomena, including the 'self', are imputed by conceptual thought. These concepts explained here and the way in which we normally view things do not correspond to each other. Phenomena are usually perceived to exist from their own nature or side, creating the illusion of an independent self-identity. This is a mistaken appearance caused by our own self-grasping. In reality everything is imputed by thought, just like the mountain in the dream. The mountain, as was earlier established, only appeared to our mind, but did not actually exist from its own side or through its own nature.

We should start to contemplate how we, ourself, are empty of inherent existence. If we practise the placement or formal meditation on emptiness, we should sit on our cushion and try to abandon all forms of negative thoughts and distractions and cultivate a wholesome state of mind. Developing the strong thought that we will now meditate on emptiness, we should first try to generate a vivid sense of 'self' or 'I'. We should develop this thought specifically. For instance, we should think of the strong sensation which appears when we are in danger such as

'I am going to fall off the cliff,'

'I am going to die'

or the strong sensation which appears when we think,

'I am angry'

or

'I am hungry.'

After generating this vivid sense of 'I', we should start to search for and try to apprehend or establish the whereabouts of this 'I'.

When searching for this 'I', there are two main possibilities. If this 'I' exists, then it must exist either in the body or the mind. Since the object of investigation is based on the 'I', and as we identify this 'I' in relation to either the body or mind, it would be illogical to search for an 'I' existing independently or separately from the body or mind.

The fact that we say 'my body' and 'my mind' shows that neither of these two is the 'I'. Because neither the body nor the mind is the 'I', therefore the collection of body and mind is not the 'I'. We should resolve that the reason why the 'I' cannot be found within the body or mind is because it is merely imputed by conceptual thought. It is because of this that the 'I' totally lacks any form of inherent existence.

After this we should fix our mind upon emptiness and remain with it single-pointedly. For those who are unfamiliar with this meditation it will be difficult to concentrate on emptiness, the object of meditation, for a long time. For this reason, when we first meditate on emptiness it is better to make the sessions short. As we gradually progress by becoming more familiar with emptiness, we can then comfortably extend our meditation sessions.

Through engaging in this meditation and gaining some experience of emptiness, we will feel that the 'I' which normally appears to our mind has been lost. Usually we cling strongly to our sense of 'I'; when we do this we apprehend an inherently existing 'I'. When we engage in meditation on emptiness, this inherently existent 'I' will be lost. If this happens our meditation can be said to be going well, drawing us closer to the actual realization of emptiness. For the time being it does not matter if we lose the 'I' because initially this acts as a powerful antidote to our previous mistaken view that the 'I' inherently exists. After we have reached this point, however, it is possible that misunderstandings may occur, leading us to fall into the extreme of nihilism.

If we fall into the extreme of nihilism after meditating on emptiness — feeling that nothing at all exists — then we should reverse our meditation and contemplate how the 'I' does exist. For example, if the 'I' does not exist, who is now thinking and making this investigation? Because the 'I' is a phenomenon it must exist. But when we investigate and try to establish its existence, it is unfindable. It is important to know that there is no contradiction between these two statements which refer respectively to the conventional and ultimate natures of the 'I'. When we understand that conventional and ultimate truth do not con-

tradict each other, we have achieved the union of the two realities. Having gained this understanding, there will then be no danger of falling into either of the two extremes: the extreme of nihilism or the extreme of belief in inherent self-existence.

Meditating on emptiness is a very powerful remedy which helps to avert our obstacles. We should therefore try to keep emptiness constantly in mind — reading, thinking, studying and meditating on it whenever the opportunity arises. This in turn will finally bring about our intuitive realization of emptiness and liberation from suffering.

CHAPTER 14

INTRODUCTION TO VAJRAYANA

This chapter will introduce the Vajrayana or Secret Mantra. The actual practice of Vajrayana will not be explained here. In order to receive teachings on Vajrayana or Tantra, one needs first to have the initiation or empowerment for the practice. Instructors are not allowed to speak about Tantra to the uninitiated. Even if instructions about Vajrayana were given, there would be no benefits if one had not received the empowerment. But a general introduction to the Tantra or Vajrayana can be given.

Nowadays some people get the impression that the Vajrayana or Secret Mantra teachings were created by Tibetan lamas. But this is not the case: the Vajrayana teachings were expounded by Shakyamuni Buddha himself. Among the teachings of the Buddha, the Secret Mantra teachings are the highest and most profound. It is the Vajrayana which represents the ultimate thought or intention of the Buddha. Buddha gave many teachings, including the Hinayana and Mahayana Sutras. These teachings are the foundation of the Vajrayana. It is upon the basis of the Sutra teachings that Secret Mantra must be practised.

Shakyamuni Buddha had countless spiritual disciples. Not all of his disciples had the same intelligence; some were very intelligent, some were of medium intelligence, and some were of low intelligence. Therefore Buddha expounded his teachings according to the different capacities and levels of intelligence of different disciples. If Buddha had taught very high teachings to those of low intelligence, this would not have been very helpful. In the same way, a child who does not know the alphabet will not benefit from receiving advanced teachings on grammar. For the beings of low intelligence, Buddha expounded the Hinayana teachings. To those of middle intelligence, Buddha gave the Mahayana Sutras in addition to the Hinayana teachings. Finally, for the advanced disciples of high intelligence, Buddha expounded the Secret Mantra or Vajrayana teachings in addition to the Hinayana and Mahayana teachings.

When Buddha taught these three different levels of teachings, he manifested different physical forms. To give the Hinayana teachings, Buddha appeared externally as a monk. When Buddha gave the Mahayana Sutra teachings he appeared as a Bodhisattva. It is said that the gods or Devas and even the spirits came to listen when he expounded the Mahayana Sutras. When Buddha taught the Vajrayana he manifested in the form of a meditational deity, called in Tibetan a Yidam. For example, when Buddha expounded the Heruka teachings he appeared in the form of Heruka (a meditational deity). The deity's form could not be perceived by ordinary human beings, but only by the special fortunate disciples known as the vajra disciples.

There was once a king called Indrabodhi who requested Buddha to give Vajrayana teachings. King Indrabodhi was very rich and powerful. He had no desire to abandon his worldly activities, but still wanted to practise Dharma and to reach Enlightenment. The king went to see Buddha and asked him if there was a teaching which he could practise without giving up his worldly pursuits and which had the power to bring him to Enlightenment quickly. Buddha then taught the king the Guhyasamaja Tantra. The Guhyasamaja or Secret Assembly teaching is the king of all Secret Mantra teachings; it is very extensive.

Vajrayana teachings flourished widely in Tibet. There were many yogis or mahasiddhas in Tibet who attained Enlightenment in one lifetime through the practice of Tantra. Even today there is a complete unbroken lineage of the transmission of the Secret Mantra teachings. All the inner experience and inner development still exists.

In order to practise Secret Mantra sincerely, one needs the appropriate empowerments. Tantric empowerments should be received from a very qualified guru or teacher. When the lama or guru grants this empowerment, it plants the seed for the practice of Secret Mantra. It creates the potential power to practise Secret Mantra successfully and to gain inner realizations. Through depending on the meditation techniques of Secret Mantra, one develops great potential power to reach Enlightenment. The empowerment is like a seed from which realizations can sprout. Without planting the seed-like empowerment there can be no sprout-like realizations.

The initiation or empowerment is the gateway to the Vajrayana practices. The great yogi Milarepa once told his disciples that if they had first trained and controlled their minds, he would grant them empowerment which was the gateway to Secret Mantra. Then he would give them the actual instructions so that they could practise or meditate on these. Thus, the empowerment is very important.

Compared to the Sutra paths, Secret Mantra is a very high or superior path. The Vajrayana is a quicker path to Enlightenment than the Sutra paths. The Tantric teachings are extremely rare and therefore it is very difficult to meet and receive pure Tantric teachings.

What is the etymology or derivation of the term 'Secret Mantra'? 'Secret' here means that the teacher should give Secret Mantra teachings only to those who have the empowerment and who have strong faith in these teachings. Secret Mantra should be kept hidden. Those who have no faith and those who have not received the empowerment should not be taught Secret Mantra. The disciples who have received empowerment should practise in secret, without displaying their practice to others.

A rich man or woman may have many precious jewels never displayed to others, but kept secretly. If these precious jewels were displayed, there would be many dangers such as thieves. Likewise, the precious Vajrayana should be kept secretly. If we have received empowerments and wish sincerely to practise Secret Mantra, we should do so privately, without display to others. If we do display our Secret Mantra practices to others, internal or external obstacles or interferences can arise. Therefore, Secret Mantra should be practised in secret.

The next word is 'Mantra'. This means mind protection. Depending on Secret Mantra practices protects our mind from ordinary appearances and conceptions. All of our ordinarily seen appearances are impure appearances. Because of impure appearances we are circling in samsara and we experience suffering. Therefore it is very important to prevent ordinary appearances. It is the practice of Secret Mantra which destroys ordinary impure appearances and protects our mind.

There are four levels of Vajrayana practice, of which the latter ones are higher than the former. The first type of Secret Mantra is called Action Tantra. The second type is called Performance Tantra. The third is Yoga Tantra and the last is the Highest Yoga Tantra. All these four yogas of Secret Mantra transform bliss into the spiritual path, but there are large differences between them. According to the different capacities of the practitioners there are different ways of transforming bliss into the spiritual path.

The practitioner of Action Tantra first tries to develop bliss by meditating on an attractive, visualized deity. The bliss which arises is the bliss of just looking at the object. This mind of bliss then meditates or concentrates on emptiness.

The Performance Tantra practitioners try to develop bliss by visualizing the attractive deity smiling or laughing. Then they try to use the bliss they develop to meditate upon emptiness and thus transform bliss into the spiritual path.

Practitioners of the third or Yoga Tantra attempt to develop bliss through touching the hands of the attractive visualized deity. When this bliss arises, the bliss meditates on emptiness and is thus transformed into the spiritual path.

In the Highest Yoga Tantra, practitioners embrace an actual consort or visualize such an embrace and try to develop bliss. By meditating on emptiness this bliss is transformed into the profound spiritual path. All of the various Tantric practices of the yogis and yoginis are based upon the mind of bodhicitta. In order to bring all sentient beings into the supreme state of Buddhahood, they practise Secret Mantra.

When the Secret Mantra practitioner develops desirous attachment, he or she never abandons this immediately. Instead, by depending on desirous attachment the practitioner tries to develop bliss. This bliss becomes transformed into the path to Enlightenment. This is taught only in Secret Mantra.

If we are very intelligent we can see that the Buddha's teachings were extremely skilful. Most of us like desirous attachment. Desirous attachment is our normal practice, so Buddha gave us a very useful method to transform our normal desirous attachment. According to Secret Mantra, Buddha never said that we should abandon our desirous attachment immediately; instead we should try to transform it into the spiritual path. This is the highest, the supreme method.

However, someone who has little understanding might find difficulties and obstacles to Vajrayana practice. Not everyone can practise Secret Mantra. People with very strong deluded minds or those with uncontrolled minds have problems in practising Secret Mantra. Initially it is very important to tame our mind by means of Hinayana and Mahayana teachings and methods. After controlling our mind, it is then very easy to practise Secret Mantra. If we are skilful in practising Tantra, life becomes very blissful and the practice leads from joy to joy. It is not a very difficult method; it transforms daily activities such as eating, sleeping, sexual desire, etc., into the path to Enlightenment.

Secret Mantra has four attributes which are not included in Sutra.

The first special attribute of Secret Mantra is the yoga of the complete purification of the place. The second attribute is the yoga of the complete purification of the body, and the third one is the yoga of the complete purification of enjoyment. Finally, there is the yoga of the complete purification of action. Any teaching which contains these four yogas is Secret Mantra.

The practitioner of Secret Mantra prevents the ordinary appearance of the place or environment. Instead, he or she visualizes the environment as a Buddha-field or as the palace (mandala) of a meditational deity. This practice of preventing the ordinary appearance is the yoga of the complete purification of the place.

The second yoga is to prevent the ordinary appearance of the gross physical body. The practitioners develop the divine pride of being a deity-Buddha. The third yoga is to prevent the ordinary appearance of one's enjoyments. Whatever one enjoys such as food and so forth is visualized as being enjoyed by the deity, as being an offering to the deity.

The fourth yoga of the complete purification of action is to prevent the ordinary appearance of one's actions and to transform whatever actions are performed into Enlightened actions. All of these practices are known as taking the results into the path. That is, the Buddhahood which will be experienced in the future is mixed into one's meditation now. This is a very special characteristic of Secret Mantra.

Secret Mantra has the power to destroy our ordinary death, ordinary intermediate state, and ordinary rebirth. By means of Secret Mantra, in place of these three ordinary states we can attain a Buddha's three bodies: the truth body, enjoyment body, and emanation body. According to Buddhism, we follow a cycle of existence in which we experience death, the intermediate or bardo state, rebirth, and then death over and over again. These three states follow one after another as in a circle or wheel. If we break a wheel at any one place it will not continue to circle. Likewise, if we prevent one of the three ordinary states of death, the intermediate state or rebirth, there will be no more cyclic existence. Secret Mantra contains special methods for transforming these three ordinary states into the spiritual path.

There are many more benefits of Secret Mantra and now we have a special opportunity if we wish to practise this method. At the present time we have the precious human form and have met the Secret Mantra teachings. Je Tsong Khapa said that the Vajrayana teachings are more rare than Buddhas. In this kalpa or aeon one thousand Buddhas will

come. Four Buddhas have already appeared in the present age, and the rest are still to come. But only three of these thousand Buddhas will teach Secret Mantra; only the fourth, the eleventh and the last Buddha will expound these rare teachings.

Many people discuss and are interested in Tantra or Secret Mantra. But only very few people practise the true, pure Secret Mantra. There are now many misconceptions about Tantra. Many people who say they are practising Secret Mantra commit immoral actions, while saying that those who keep moral discipline are following a lower path and not practising Secret Mantra. Some people even become teachers of Secret Mantra and think that they have high spiritual development, but they perform very negative actions such as sexual misconduct. They pretend that they are practising Secret Mantra in this way. Giving the name 'Secret Mantra' to these bad actions and pretending to be a teacher of Secret Mantra is very dangerous.

Superficially, it may seem as though Secret Mantra and desirous attachment have a connection, but in reality they are totally different. For those who are very unskilful in practising Secret Mantra, their practice becomes a cause of lower rebirth. Instead of using Secret Mantra to attain a higher rebirth or Enlightenment, those who misuse the practices descend to lower rebirths. If teachers teach bad behaviour to their disciples in the name of Secret Mantra, both the teacher and the disciples may fall into lower rebirths. Because many wrong ideas can develop about Secret Mantra, even Buddhas never teach Secret Mantra to everyone.

Why do we need to practise Secret Mantra? We need to practise Secret Mantra now because it is very hard to find again in the future. Secret Mantra is an extremely powerful method: it is a very swift path to Enlightenment. Secret Mantra is the essence of the teachings of Shakyamuni Buddha.

GLOSSARY

(Sans.) or (Tib.) indicates a word of Sanskrit or Tibetan origin.

Actions and their effects	The process through which wholesome actions produce happiness and unwholesome ones produce suffering: karma
Arhat (Sans.)	Literally: foe destroyer; one who has destroyed the foe of delusions and attained liberation from cyclic existence.
Arya (Sans.)	Literally: a superior being; someone who has attained a direct perception of ultimate truth
Asanga (Sans.)	A Buddhist master noted for his realization of compassion; active in India around the fourth to fifth centuries AD.
Atisha (Sans.)	Indian Buddhist master who came to Tibet in the eleventh century to spread Buddhist teachings.
Bodhicitta (Sans.)	The altruistic mind of Enlightenment; the continuous and spontaneous wish to gain full Enlightenment for the benefit of all sentient beings.
Bodhisattva (Sans.)	Someone who posseses the mind of Enlightenment or bodhicitta; a being on the path to full Enlightenment.
Bodhisattva vows	Vows taken with the bodhicitta motivation in which one promises to practise the six perfections — generosity, moral discipline, patience, joyous effort, concentration and wisdom.
Buddha (Sans.)	A fully Enlightened being; someone who has attained complete liberation from suffering and omniscience; a being who has perfected all good qualities and removed every gross and subtle obscura-

	tion veiling the mind.
Buddha Shakyamuni (Sans.)	The founder of the Buddhist tradition; lived and taught in India during the sixth and fifth centuries BC.
Buddhahood	The state of full Enlightenment; the final goal of the Mahayana practitioner.
Compassion	A mind which wishes others to be free from suffering.
Cyclic existence	The cycle of uncontrolled birth, death and rebirth; samsara. Cyclic existence results from actions produced by delusions.
Delusion	A mind which disturbs one's mental peace.
Deva (Sans.)	In general, a kind of being of a higher aspect than humans.
Dharma (Sans.)	The spiritual teachings of Shakyamuni Buddha; the inner realizations which hold one back from suffering.
Empowerment	Authorization to practise the generation of oneself as a deity-Buddha and to receive teachings about Secret Mantra.
Energy winds	Inner currents of air which control physical functions and serve as the bases or mounts of consciousness. It is said that consciousness is mounted on wind like a rider on a horse.
Emptiness	The lack of inherent existence of all phenomena; ultimate truth.
Enlightenment	The state of eternal peace and the realization of a foe destroyer or a Buddha.
Equanimity	A state of even-mindedness; an unbiased mind toward others.
Generic image	An appearance of an object appearing directly to conception.
Geshe (Tib.)	A title achieved through studying great Buddhist treatises.
Great compassion	The mind of compassion directed toward all sentient beings.
Guru (Sans.)	Teacher; spiritual guide.

Hinayana (Sans.)	Buddhist spiritual paths which emphasize individual liberation from the sufferings of cyclic existence; the Lesser Vehicle.
Inherent existence	Independent existence or existence from its own side.
Ishvara (Sans.)	One of the main gods worshipped by Hindus.
Je Tsong Khapa (Tib.)	Great Tibetan teacher and revitalizer of Buddhism who lived in the fourteenth and fifteenth centuries AD; an emanation of the Buddha Manjushri — the embodiment of all the Buddhas' wisdom.
Karma (Sans.)	Literally: actions. See 'Actions and their effects'.
Lama (Tib.)	Tibetan title for a spiritual master.
Liberation	Freedom from the sufferings of cyclic existence; nirvana.
Love	A mind which wishes others to have happiness.
Lower realms	The unpleasant states of existence in samsara below the human realm. These include the animal, hungry spirit and hell realms.
Mahayana (Sans.)	Inner paths motivated by bodhicitta; the Great Vehicle.
Mantra (Sans.)	Literally: mind protection; mantra protects one's mind from ordinary appearances and conceptions.
Marpa (Tib.)	A Tibetan translator of Buddhist texts; the guru of Milarepa.
Meditation	Placing and focusing the mind on any wholesome object.
Mental factor	A particular function of a primary mind.
Merit	The wholesome forces and tendencies accumulated through virtuous actions of body, speech or mind.
Milarepa (Tib.)	One of the main disciples of Marpa. He attained full Enlightenment in one lifetime.

Mind	That which is formless, clear and cognizing.
Nagarjuna (Sans.)	Great Buddhist sage who lived around the second century AD, and was the chief propagator of the Middle Way philosophy of emptiness.
Nirvana (Sans.)	The state beyond sorrow; personal or self-liberation sometimes called the lower nirvana to distinguish it from full Enlightenment.
Ordinary being	Someone who has not realized emptiness directly.
Samsara (Sans.)	See 'Cyclic existence'.
Sangha (Sans.)	The spiritual community of those who have taken ordination or Bodhisattva vows.
Secret Mantra	See 'Tantra'.
Self-grasping	A mistaken mind which conceives the inherent existence of 'self' of persons or other phenomena.
Sentient being	A being who has mental obstacles and obscurations.
Shakyamuni (Sans.)	Title of Gautama Buddha meaning sage of the Shakya clan.
Sutra (Sans.)	Buddha's common discourses.
Tantra (Sans.)	Buddha's secret teachings and practices.
Thing (or functioning thing)	That which is able to perform a function.
Three Jewels	The Buddha, Dharma and Sangha; the three objects of Buddhist refuge.
Tranquil abiding	A meditative concentration which possesses special suppleness of body and mind.
Vajrayana (Sans.)	Uncommon vehicle leading to full Enlightenment.
Vasubandhu (Sans.)	Great Buddhist philosopher and logician who lived around the fourth to fifth centuries AD; author of the *Abidharmakosa* (Treasury of Phenomenology).
Wisdom	A mind which correctly understands its object and eliminates doubts.

Yoga (Sans.)	A method to lead beings to any actual spiritual practice.
Yogi (Feminine: yogini) (Sans.)	A person who has achieved special spiritual experience in dependence upon any yoga.